Praise for *Spiritual Transformation: Reclaiming Our Birthright*

You hold in your hands a precious gift, a treasure whose value cannot be overstated. This book offers you a road map to the journey of your soul that will help you find the core of what it means to live an abundant and free life.

    —John Woodall, MD, Psychiatrist
       Sandy Hook, CT

A young Iranian student, an ardent follower of the Bahá'í Faith, is swept off her feet, falls in in love with an African American in the '60s and is thrown into the belly of racism in the American South. It's a fantastic story of her life's journey to self-discovery. Drawing from her life experiences and therapy practice, she offers an amazing blend of psychotherapy tools and spiritual teachings, offering enlightenment to anyone searching for joy and self-fulfillment regardless of race, gender, or background.

    —Sophia Bracy Harris, Retired Executive Director
       Federation of Child Care Centers of Alabama

A beautifully well-written, easily understandable, and compelling book that can be used as a powerful and practical guide for the spiritual and personal growth in the journey of life. Using her own life events and experiences, she offers a guided road map in finding our own individual self within—a self that is more loved, empowered, spiritual, and accepted. A self that is ready to emerge and burst out with contentment, joy, and abundance of love for self and others.

    —Arefeh Langkilde, MA Psychology, EdS Specialist in Education

Spiritual Transformation: Reclaiming Our Birthright offers a unique pathway to a new world order. Fafar weaves together the forces of spirituality, religion, professional expertise, and profound lived experience, and applies these to issues of personal relationships that challenge us all. Her book offers wise and tested practical strategies and deep insights bathed in her love of humanity and belief in its inherent goodness.

    This work offers the gift to reclaim civil society through the transformation of our personal relationships.

    —Di James, Founding Director
       Family Action Centre of the University of Newcastle, Australia

This book is one of those that you cannot put down, and keeps you asking what happens next! As a therapist, Fafar becomes a beacon of light in group and individual sessions, helping us to see our true selves through her own transparency and authentic modeling, and gives us hope that being truly happy is possible. Reading her book was a refresher course that brought back some forgotten concepts that I will use in my own work with my clients.

—Mahin Pouryaghma, PhD, LPC

Reading through *Spiritual Transformation* is like reviewing the most important lessons and experiences of my life—with the guidance that has come from her Faith and wisdom. Her loving and sweet voice is a "bridge over troubled waters." She colors in this "world of dust" with meaning and beauty. This book is an offering of love to each reader seeking a roadmap to their personal transformation and a service toward the advancement of a world of peace, joy, and balance for us all.

—Paula Bailey, Registered Nurse on a high-risk obstetrics unit

Reading Fafar's book was wonderful for me. I was the lucky typist of the manuscript and so I was able to take it in by reading and also kinesthetically by typing. For a kinesthetic learner, this is a special treat! The reader of this book knows they are being loved. We feel loved by her personal sharing of struggles, pain, and her own inner process. We feel loved by her humor, expressed throughout her book—and we feel her love through her openness and authenticity.

—Annie Janus, MS, Clinical Counseling

We all are living through a very stressful and challenging chapter in the history of humanity. In describing her own search for self-understanding, Fafar interweaves the teachings of the Bahá'í Faith with psychotherapy in a way that beautifully illuminates the fact that it is not selfish or narcissistic to value, and to understand, our own selves. On the contrary, it is our purpose and our right to recognize our dignity and nobility, and to achieve an awareness of our spiritual reality. This book has made me laugh and cry; its being written from a woman's perspective made it especially meaningful for me. Thank you, Fafar, for your wisdom—and for your honest sharing of your own struggles and search for self-knowledge, which is ultimately spiritual transformation.

—Ruth Rogers, Interior Architectural Designer

Fafar's work helps me keep understanding the role of spirit on earth. The way she brings life to the conception of us as spiritual beings in a physical form took my breath away over and over as I read! *Spiritual Transformation* has applications for all who seek both emotional health and spiritual truth; it also shows us how to live with and challenge the physical and structural realities of disease and oppression. What a gift to the world!

— Valerie Batts, VP of Training & Development and Founding Director, VISIONS, Inc.

Farzaneh Guillebeaux has written a book that is not only grounded in practical, useful information; it also inspires you at your core. She allows us to journey through some of the most private and painful areas of her life, and through her transparency we as clinicians, professionals and the common everyday person are given a front seat as she traverses through the experiential development of self and others. As a Christian, this book encourages me even as it presents challenges in my way of thinking, living, and being.

— Pastor Leon Corder, MA, Counseling Psychology

In her book, Farzaneh Guillebeaux interweaves an unguarded account of her own journey to knowing and loving herself; practical strategies and examples grounded in years of experience as a therapist; and a wealth of invocations from the Baháʼí writings to pursue one's own spiritual transformation. This combination of science and the spiritual persuasively dismisses any idea that self-care and understanding are mere "navel-gazing," and instead poses them as essential tools on the path to know and love God. The resulting tapestry is one which compels — and empowers — the reader to embark on their own journey to know and nurture their own self.

— Jen Azordegan, PhD, Educational Psychology

Fafar speaks the unspoken and confronts the hidden that many of us have experienced. By sharing her own life struggles, she models how vulnerability can lead to an authentic and empowered self. She makes clear that the work is gradual and is the total responsibility of the individual. It isn't easy.

I once heard that the therapist could only take their clients as far as she has gone in her own abilities and self-growth. Fafar Guillebeaux has had many opportunities in life to become consecrated and claim her birthright.

— Lisa Puzon, DT, Psychology

The awakening of the soul is the most important journey each of us will ever take. It is not for the faint of heart. Yet, for those courageous enough to enter the transforming fires of suffering and let God cook us into who we came here to be, the rewards are great. I found this journey profoundly shared in Farzaneh Guillebeaux's moving memoir, *Spiritual Transformation: Reclaiming Our Birthright*. By her willingness to share her own dark times—from her father's suicide, the threat of loss of her marriage, to her battle with CFS and cancer—and her deep faith in God, her thirst for understanding took her on an unexpected journey of awakening a deep spiritual transformation within herself, her family, and beloved friends. Her love of life, people, and God sees her through over and over as she grows and allows her soul to be polished by life. I found it a particularly valuable gift for those of the Bahá'í faith or curious about it, since it offers a unique inward window into the power of its teachings, although people from all walks of life will be touched by her journey and the gems of insights she shares along the way.

— Michael Brant DeMaria, PhD, Integrative Psychologist, bestselling author, and four-time Grammy-nominated musician

Spiritual Transformation

Reclaiming Our Birthright

By

Farzaneh Guillebeaux

Under no circumstances shall any of the information provided herein be construed as medical advice of any kind.

Spiritual Transformation:
Reclaiming Our Birthright
Farzaneh Guillebeaux

Copyright © 2020 Farzaneh Guillebeaux

All rights reserved. Except as permitted under U.S. Copyright Act of 1976, no part of this publication may be reproduced, distributed, or transmitted in any form or by any means, or stored in a database or retrieval system, without the prior written permission of the publisher.

Published by Together Editing Press
855 El Camino Real Suite 13A-190, Palo Alto, CA 94301, United States
www.togetherediting.com

ISBN-13: 978-1-939698-04-9
Printed in the United States of America

Editing and design by Together Editing & Design
www.togetherediting.com

First Edition: November 2020

9 8 7 6 5 4 3 2 1

Cover design by Lisa Puzon
Original artwork: Annie Janus

As for the spiritual perfections they
are man's birthright and belong to him alone…
—'Abdu'l-Bahá, *Paris Talks*

For my Papa,

Hujjat'u'lláh Rabbání,

who loved the Faith with ardent, unbounded,

exuberant, and unabashed passion!

Contents

Foreword	vii
Preface	xi
Part I: Introduction	1
What Led Me to Therapy	3
The Practice of Psychotherapy: "I Did It My Way…"	14
Becoming an Author	20
Part II: Some Theoretical Foundations for Spiritual Transformation	31
The Three Basic Questions	33
Options for Making Change Happen	36
Getting to Know Me through Ego States	40
Evolutionary Nature of Transformation	48
Part III: Tools for Transformation	53
The Divine Owner's Manual: Who God Says I Am	55
The "Okay Corral" — Another Vital Practical Tool for Transformation	59
FAM: Feelings as Messengers	69
Strokes: Emotional Fuel for Life	90
Part IV: Putting Everything into Practice	101
The Role of Tests and Difficulties on the Journey Toward Wholeness and Authenticity	103
Fruits of CFS	112
"Being Happy, a Delectable Duty"	123
"What's Love Got to Do with It?"	141
Afterword	151
Appendix	159
Acknowledgements	161
Central Figures of the Bahá'í Faith	163
Suggested Reading List	165
Bibliography	167
About the Author	173

Foreword

You hold in your hands a precious gift, a treasure whose value cannot be overstated. This book offers you a road map to the journey of your soul that will help you find the core of what it means to live an abundant and free life. We become fellow wayfarers on this journey with Farzaneh Guillebeaux (Fafar, as her friends know her) as she shares with us her own unfolding along this path.

There are three things that make this book the powerful tool for self-unfolding that it is. The first is the primal generative power of the Writings of Bahá'u'lláh that are this journey's key reference point. The second is that it uses the formidable tool of Transactional Analysis, a common sense and easily communicable school of psychotherapy, as a framework for our journey. The generative and transformational principles outlined by Bahá'u'lláh become accessible and familiar to us through the lens of Transactional Analysis (TA). As a psychiatrist, I find that TA adds fresh perspective and offers us tools to begin our own transformation as described by Bahá'u'lláh: these tools help us operationalize the transformation that Bahá'u'lláh calls us to. With these tools in the hands of this wise and kind wayfarer, Fafar herself is the third and perhaps critical element of the transformative power of this book. She has read the book of her own inner self and reflected deeply on the realities of our nature as described by Bahá'u'lláh using the lens of TA.

By showing us her own journey of self-reflection and transformation, Fafar demonstrates the skills of the mind and heart that are necessary to examine the limiting and often hurtful assumptions we make about our lives. The "vain imaginings" and "idle fancies" described by Bahá'u'lláh as the main obstacles to our growth are cast into relief by the language of TA that describes the assumptions—the "scripts"—that are formed in our early life and distort our perception of our enormous capacity. These assumptions cloak our motivation to reach for more in life in shame or fear, and taint the richness that might be ours in our interactions with others.

Carl Jung once said that we spend the first third of our lives developing an identity largely shaped by our surroundings. The next third of life is examining the false elements of these assumptions that make up that identity and cause us unnecessary pain; hopefully, in the last third of our lives we can then enjoy a state of inner freedom from these assumptions in which we create our own joy and meaning. The chief obstacles to this progressive growth are the fear and shame we take on early in life that are based on false assumptions about our inmost self. We flee from self-reflection because we fear that these assumptions might prove to be true — that we will be exposed for the shameful and unworthy person we most fear that we are.

It is these very assumptions that prove to be false. Bahá'u'lláh tells us, as do all the Founders of the world's great religious systems, that the ground of all existence is love and mercy: out of grace we are forgiven and held in the gentle hands of compassion, no matter what our circumstances. Our truest inner nature is noble and wonderous. We can, as Fredrich Nietzsche said, live in a state of "amor fati." We can learn to "love fate" no matter what it has unfolded in our lives, without being condemned to a state of constant shame, guilt, humiliation, and fear.

I write this foreword to Fafar's book from Newtown, Connecticut, close to the anniversary of the tragic murder of 20 six-year-old children and six of their teachers in 2012. The bitterness of that day and the enduring effects it has had on the town are immeasurable. Such tragedy is not uncommon in an increasingly violent and chaotic world; this kind of senseless violence can be traced back to individuals who have never felt that the world is a safe place for them. There are far too many who feel the world repeatedly reinforces the sense of shame and humiliation they carry about life. They have not yet been freed from the "vain imaginings" of these assumptions about life, and this very shame and humiliation then fuel rage, fear, and violence in countless forms. This reality makes the message Farzaneh Guillebeaux brings to us all the more urgent. We must, as the Greek poet Aeschylus said, "tame the savageness of man and make gentle the life of the world."

We must help each other quiet the inner voices of self-condemnation we all harbor. We urgently need the healing and peace-inducing balm of the knowledge of our own dignity, our own worthy acceptance into the world — and our legitimate place in it. The real truth is that we are beings of love: we are noble and necessary players in the story of the unfoldment of human potential. We are one human family put here to help and nurture each other in the struggles of life. Despite the enduring grief at senseless loss that fate or human depravity mete out to us, we can yet find an "amor fati," a "love of fate" that is grounded in our own assurance of the ever-present and encompassing grace that embraces and flows between us all as we help each other through the course of life's sufferings.

We cannot be this for ourselves and each other until we have rid ourselves of the false narratives we tell ourselves about who we are and what our lives can be. For this, we need more than ever the clarion call of Bahá'u'lláh and tools like Transactional Analysis to help us move toward that vision.

Most of all, we need guides who can show us the path to truth. We need souls who have not been afraid to look deeply within themselves to face the fears—the doubts and misconceptions we all carry—in order to come out the other end as transformed and willing helpers of others on that journey. We need living embodiments of the truth of this type of transformation. Farzaneh Guillebeaux is such a person and this book is the embodiment of that transformation in her life. The truths contained in this book are the truths that can set us all free.

John Woodall, MD, Psychiatrist
Sandy Hook, CT

Preface

This book has unfolded through its own evolutionary process for the past 29 years! From the beginning, the impetus for writing it has been to bring together the overarching—and sometimes overwhelming—spiritual guidance from the Bahá'í Writings (scriptures) with the practical theory and practice from psychotherapy in order to facilitate the process of spiritual growth and transformation that is the primary purpose of our earthly life. There have been multiple reasons for the long gestation period and birth of this book. On the surface, I could sum up the delay with "life intervened and interfered." And this would be true enough! There is also the fact that 23 out of the 29 years I have been living with the severely limiting reality of Chronic Fatigue Syndrome (CFS). However, the most profound and perhaps mysterious reason has been the contributing role and function of the intervening years. If this book had been written 29 years ago, it would have been mostly theoretical. The events of my life, which often appeared as trials and difficulties, provided me with the opportunity to put the spiritual guidance and therapeutic theory into practice. As a result, most of what I share here has been tested and tried in the laboratory of my own life! From the book's inception, my heart's desire was to eagerly invite the reader to awaken to herself/himself with joy and curiosity, stressing that ignorance of "self" does not constitute humility or "selflessness!" Through my own painstaking journey, I have concluded that the "self" cannot be known without a loving, attentive, and patient attitude toward it.

I also realized that the process of spiritual transformation is continuous, complex, and often breathtakingly challenging. As an Iranian woman and a fifth-generation Bahá'í, it would be an understatement to say that neither my cultural nor my religious (in the narrow sense that I had once defined it) background had prepared me to embrace "therapy"! In retrospect, when my life circumstances forced me to seek therapy, a brand-new world was, luckily, opened to me.

It was a thrilling discovery to realize that basic and fundamental changes in one's character were possible and that there was practical guidance to facilitate the process. I have come to regard it as a true Eureka moment in which the proverbial light came on: *the comprehension that a harmonious marriage of spiritual truth and practical psychotherapeutic theories was not only possible, but also highly desirable.* It was personally confirming to experience and appreciate one of the basic principles of the Bahá'í Faith—the essential harmony between science and religion. It became infinitely clear to me that if I were to consciously engage in this difficult, confounding, and often painful process of spiritual transformation, I needed all the help I could get from both science and religion.

Although the spiritual truths and guidance are primarily from the Bahá'í Writings, this book is by no means for Bahá'ís only; its message is universal. If you are a follower of any of the other major world religions, the Bahá'í Faith affirms and is the spiritual truths revealed in all other Holy Books; briefly stated, Bahá'ís believe that there is, and has ever been, only one Creator. Because we believe that the Author of all the Holy Books, such as the Torah, the New Testament, the Bhagavad Gita, the Zenda Vesta, the Quran, and the Bahá'í Writings, is the one and only God, we accept and revere the Founders of all Religions as One. There is no competition, only completion. Even if you are an agnostic or atheist—and I believe that many enlightened souls have taken refuge in those categories based on their justifiable disillusionment with what has been and is being done in the name of religion—and believe that there might be more to us than our physical body limited by our five senses, you may find parts of this book to be useful in your daily life.

In the book there are references made to the Báb, Bahá'u'lláh, 'Abdu'l-Bahá, the Guardian, and the Universal House of Justice. For the explanations of these titles and their respective stations, please refer to the Appendix under Central Figures of the Faith. For more information about the Bahá'í Faith, please refer to the Appendix, as well as www.bahai.org.

When it comes to the use of pronouns, except for the second paragraph in the Introduction, I have chosen to alternate randomly between all pronouns.

The book is laid out in parts. The first section gives you a brief account of my history and my journey toward therapy and therapeutic work. The second lays out theoretical underpinnings for practices I've found useful in my ongoing struggle for self-knowledge and spiritual transformation. In the third section, I describe in detail some of the therapeutic practices I've employed in my self-work as well as in work with my clients, while the fourth part concludes with joyful overarching Bahá'í themes. My ultimate, highest wish would be fulfilled if this book is of assistance to you, even in a small measure, on your own journey toward wholeness and spiritual transformation.

Part I
Introduction

What Led Me to Therapy

The Fireside (informal, introductory meeting for people who seek information about the Bahá'í Faith) guests were gradually leaving, with one or two lingerers who were helping carry cups and plates to the kitchen. It had been a successful meeting with about 15 people, five or six of whom were seekers. As the last person left our cozy apartment in Smyrna, Georgia, I was sitting down, exhausted, reviewing the meeting and thinking about the next day's activities, when to my utter amazement and terror I realized that I could not move a muscle. My fear was doubled when I attempted to call Jack, my husband, to help me—but I could not utter a sound. Sitting there helpless and dumbfounded for what seemed like a long time, I was presented with an array of helpful explanations by my ever-alert mind: "You've finally done it….What's the matter with you…I always knew you didn't quite have it….Probably God is punishing you for ____ (here I was presented with multiple choices, all of which seemed equally plausible, such as not being a good enough Bahá'í, not being a worthy enough mother to my one-year-old baby, not being a loving enough daughter to my widowed mother, nor truly committing to my graduate studies, not being selfless enough)."

Before I had a chance to plead guilty to all the charges in this imagined "spiritual" court martial, the proceedings were interrupted by my husband, who had come looking for me. My apparent paralysis continued for a few more minutes as he carried me to the bedroom, where I finally regained my speech and, in frightened confusion, struggled to share my experience with him. He, characteristically in times of crisis, stalwartly arose to the challenging task of presenting his own set of plausible explanations, which were much kinder than mine; they finally comforted me into a dull sleep. That night in 1972, at the age of 30, I mark as the beginning of my conscious spiritual journey.

The next day I woke up in a state of what I now know to be akin to clinical depression. Above all, I felt a great void and a sense of purposelessness. I seemed to be drained of all motivation. I remember thinking that I was a composite of various roles: wife, mother, daughter, active Bahá'í, graduate student, none of which I felt I was adequately fulfilling. (I also felt alone and guilty for having these thoughts and feelings.) My visual image was of me standing in the middle of a circle with various people and demands reaching out to snatch bits and pieces of me, with my predominant thought being, "I have failed, I have nothing else to give."

As I now look back at the 30-year-old me, I am filled with sadness and compassion for the young woman who anxiously tried to do it all well, and blamed herself mercilessly for any real or imagined inadequacies. The facts of my life then were as follows: I was enrolled full time in graduate school getting a Master's degree in French literature, having earned a BA and a secondary-school teaching certificate five years earlier; I taught four of those years in an all-girls Catholic high school in Asheville, North Carolina, until our move to Smyrna, Georgia in 1971. I had majored in French and became a teacher not because I had a burning desire to do either one so much as a lack of a yearning desire to do much else, primarily, and I had been told that I had an aptitude for languages. I had learned Turkish and English when I went pioneering to Turkey with my family at the age of 13.[1]

But—back to my life in Georgia. To help pay for my degree, I also worked as a graduate assistant 12-15 hours a week at Georgia State University's Language Laboratory, and I spent an average of two to three hours per day commuting to and from campus. One of the things that allowed me to do all this was that two years after my beloved father's unforeseen death, my mother had come to live with us. This move was both a blessing and a challenge. Naturally, I was pleased to provide a home for my mother, but there was also much tension from time to time. Having left home at 20 to come to the States for education, I had met my husband, gotten married, and established a home. Now my mother, having lost her husband and her home, was coming to live in my home. These dynamics alone, I now realize, would have been sufficient to cause some legitimate problems and rituals of passage. In those days, however, I simply felt baffled, unhappy, and guilty. Any uneasiness or conflict I felt toward my mother I attributed to my own "selfishness" and lack of spirituality, despite my husband's frequent valiant efforts to make me realize that I needed to be more just to myself and not carry guilt for things that were not my fault.

---

[1] Bahá'ís are encouraged to disperse throughout the world to deliver the message of the Bahá'í Faith. This traveling to different areas is called *pioneering*.

Then there were all the Bahá'í activities, many of which — had I given myself permission to admit — were not bringing me much joy. In fact, feeling joyful did not seem to be a legitimate desire; instead, it appeared to be a mandate that read, "The more you do for the Cause the more joyful you ought to feel, and if you don't feel joy, it's your own fault; you're either not doing enough or not praying hard enough." Our calendar was marked months in advance, every weekend filled with activities, most of which I felt, as a Bahá'í, I should do. Additionally, there was an abundance of very vocal and super-active Bahá'ís who were not only "clear" about what they ought to do, but generously shared their chaotic vision of how others should serve as well. In retrospect, I see that the more I passively allowed other Bahá'ís to dictate how I ought to serve, feel, or be, the more dispirited and resentful I became.

Once again, back to the facts. Soon, I had all but ignored the alarm my system had sounded through the momentary shutdown or paralysis; though I may have somewhat reduced my Bahá'í activities with encouragement from my beloved and insightful Bahá'í role models, Bill and Bunny Tucker, who were visiting us during their return from their pioneering post in Jamaica. After witnessing the frantic pace of our life for a few days, and probably sensing my unhappiness, Bill gallantly volunteered to provide doctor's orders for me to slow down, even though he was an optometrist!

We stayed in Smyrna for another year, during which I completed my course work and passed my day-long written and two-hour oral comprehensive exams in French literature. This timeframe coincided with the termination of Jack's Atlanta job and the beginning of his new job, which necessitated our move to Montgomery, Alabama. Since Jack is an African American, we could not legally be married in his hometown of Asheville, North Carolina; it would be two more years before the laws were changed (*Loving v. Virginia*, 1967). In 1965, we could live there as a couple, but could not get married. That became the source of our bounty; since we had to leave the state to get married, we decided to go to Illinois to be married in the Bahá'í House of Worship in Wilmette. As an interracial couple, we used to joke about never living in Mississippi or Alabama, but somehow by November 1974, the move to Alabama felt right to both of us. For one thing (although I would only admit it to myself and Jack, and even then with a bit of guilt), I was relieved to be leaving our super-active Bahá'í setting, where I obviously felt unwilling or incapable of determining my own level of involvement.

Life in Montgomery revealed the immediate advantages of a slower pace: much less time spent in traffic and a reduced amount of Bahá'í activity. Another possible side effect of the decrease of frenzied activity was having time to notice or admit that all was not well with our marital relationship. There again I had made certain and not altogether sound assumptions that if two people choose each other out of love and attraction, as well as shared a love of God, and made a commitment to serve the Faith, all should continue to go well in their marital life. Even though there had been many ups and downs in our relationship, I held on to a naive and, in retrospect, blind and recalcitrant stance that I could work things out. (After all, my name meant the "wise one"; I had always been directly or indirectly praised for being intuitive, insightful, and wise.)

Therefore, in the tenth year of our marriage, when Jack told me that he did not feel fulfilled and happy in the relationship (and was not even sure about the Will of God relative to our togetherness), I felt confused, stunned, and devastated. For the first time in my life I felt totally helpless, powerless, and full of despair. It just wasn't supposed to go like this! I felt betrayed — not just by Jack, but by God as well. There was also the thought that God was somehow punishing me for a crime for which I had accused and found myself guilty for several years. My crime: when I left Iran in 1963, my family had, with great financial sacrifice (my part was winning a full scholarship, which paid for room and board) sent me to the United States for a college education with the expectation, at least in my own mind, that I would return afterward to Iran and miraculously rescue my family from their financial plight. After all, my beloved father, in obedience to the Guardian, had taken us pioneering to Turkey in 1954. The details of some of the failed financial plans are beyond this discussion; suffice it to say that months after my father had severed ties with his last financial base in Tehran by selling his once prosperous pharmacy, the Turkish government, without any explanation, decided to evict the five Iranian pioneer families residing in Izmir, Turkey, in 1960.

For the next three years, until my departure to the United States, I watched my broken-hearted father, who had not anticipated returning to Iran, try to re-establish himself in business without much capital and with even less hope. Unable to re-establish himself as a pharmacist due to many legal complications, he was finally able to get a small business selling notions and other odds and ends. This outcome, in very class-conscious Iranian society, was humiliation itself! My father's distress was compounded by a sense of failure for even being back in Tehran. A perceptive relative, on a visit from her pioneering post, described my father as "a caged lion" in his tiny notions store.

Since my education in an American school in Izmir had been interrupted by our eviction from Turkey, my parents were insistent that I should continue my education in the American school in Tehran in spite of the prohibitive cost. This too was in obedience to a statement from the Beloved Guardian to my father on the last day of our pilgrimage in February 1957, that "The children should learn Turkish and English and later teach in those languages." Therefore, upon graduation and winning a scholarship to a Presbyterian college in Asheville, I was put on an airplane and sent to my new life in the United States. It was clear to my father that he should somehow manage to get a ticket and put me on the plane with only $50.00 in my pocket.

I returned to Iran for a visit in 1967, two years after marrying Jack with whole-hearted consent and blessings from my parents. Meanwhile, my parents' financial troubles had continued to worsen. They had sent my brother, Fariborz, back to Turkey in 1965 to pursue his college education at the American University in Ankara. The little notions store was far from able to meet their expenses, a great part of which was medical treatment for my mother's chronic health problems. I found out later that my father, in his efforts to make ends meet, had to borrow money from relatives and friends. On February 17, 1969, apparently convinced that there was no other way out of his plight, my father took his own life. He was 52 years old.

It was years later, through the process of therapy, that I was able to discover the short and long-term effects of my father's death in all areas of my life, in all of my relationships, and above all in my relationship with God. In the immediate aftermath of his death I went to Iran, broken-hearted and confused, while trying to be brave for my mother. I tried to bring some closure to my father's business affairs, then helped my mother settle in Turkey with my brother. The plan was that they would both join us in the States upon the completion of my brother's studies. In accordance with my father's written request, my mother sent a letter to the Universal House of Justice asking for prayers of forgiveness for my father and the progress of his soul.

It was only upon my return to the United States in April 1969 that I felt the full impact of this loss, which manifested in my seemingly unbearable sadness and confusion as to how a devoted Bahá'í like my father would take his own life, my worry about the condition of his soul, and the beginnings of guilt—that somehow I should have been able to prevent this. Later, in therapy, I came to learn that these feelings are consistent with other survivors of an accidental death or a suicide. At that time, I only felt fragile and alone with my sadness, fear, and confusion.

As I look back now, I see that there were three events that brought much-needed solace and spiritual healing to my heart. The first was an early morning dream in which my father came to my house beaming with joy. In the dream I had just ironed his shirt, which seemed to have pleased him. He implied to me that all was well now and that I should not be concerned. I woke up feeling comforted and tranquil.

The second blessing, which I now gratefully recognize as a direct gift from God, was hosting the Beloved Hand of the Cause, Mr. 'Alí-Akbar Furútan, in July 1969 for a week in our tiny apartment in Asheville. He was teaching at a summer school in Black Mountain, North Carolina, and when Auxiliary Board Member Dr. William Tucker and I met him at the Asheville airport, he chose to honor me with his blessed presence. During the week, he, who had known our family for a long time, was like a nurturing spiritual father in whom I could confide all my fears, questions, and sadness. Sometimes he would share his memories of the Beloved Guardian; other times, he would patiently answer my questions. Often, with his magnificent sense of humor, he would tell me jokes in order to cheer me up.

The third blessing that happened during the week with Mr. Furútan was the arrival of the letter from the Universal House of Justice in response to my mother's request. In his rather lengthy suicide note, my father had expressed his love for Bahá'u'lláh, acknowledged the wrongness of taking his own life, and requested that my mother write to the House of Justice to beg for their prayers that he would be forgiven. Mr. Furútan lovingly pointed out that after the receipt of that letter, if I continued to be restless and agitated, it would be a sign of ingratitude and a cause of sadness to my father's soul. I will be forever grateful to Mr. Furútan for his gift of love, wisdom, and spiritual nurturance at such a critical juncture in my spiritual life. These blessings enabled me to reach a semblance of closure and to form a scab on the gaping open wound caused by the death of my beloved father. Again, as I later realized, there were many questions and concerns in my heart and mind, but at the time I would not even have been able to articulate them, let alone look for answers. Therefore, I continued with my life the best way I could.

So, once again we return to Montgomery, circa 1975 or 1976, at the lowest point in our marital life. As often happens, tests come in a series: right around this time, Jack lost his job and was often withdrawn and depressed. The image imprinted in my mind from that period is Jack sprawled on the living room floor, seemingly interminably listening to Ray Charles, Dinah Washington, and Harry Chapin. Because of our wounded and ailing relationship, we had tall and thick walls that prevented us from being a refuge for each other.

Actually, when I think back, I had used, really misused, the "fortress for well-being" (a metaphor for marriage; see Bahá'u'lláh, in *Bahá'í Prayers*, 116) not as a refuge, but as a hideaway where Jack was to protect me from the "big bad world," myself, and ultimately, from "Big Bad God." And although none of this had been consciously owned or formulated, let alone articulated, Jack must have felt the crushing burden of this impossible role. This too I remember as a vignette; at a later point in a therapist's office, having bemoaned Jack's loss of interest in the relationship and declaring my state of confusion for how I was being paid back for all my love, Jack's exasperated response was that my love had begun to feel like a noose around his neck. Now, both my pathetic pleas and his desperate response seem poignantly funny, but at the time, I felt totally betrayed, victimized, and justifiably angry.

I have often referred to the events of that period as a divine earthquake of just the right magnitude to leave me uprooted (since I had rooted myself in quicksand that sooner or later would have shifted anyhow), helpless, and in despair. I was left face-to-face with me, and ultimately with my relationship to God. I remember somewhere along this juncture having an honest, albeit scary, conversation with God in which I stated that I didn't know if I was being punished for being selfish in regard to my parents or any other wrongdoing, and I didn't understand why my husband didn't love me anymore. I was very scared and confused that I didn't want to serve the Faith (in the narrow sense that I had defined service at that point), but I did know one thing: that I could not, would not, force myself back into what for me had become a meaningless, frenzied Bahá'í activity scene. Even the thought of it felt like spiritual suicide. I felt that even if I succeeded in forcing myself into that straitjacket, in a few years I would either die, lose my mind, or have to resign from the Faith. My conclusion was that since a result of any of the above eventualities meant there would be one less Bahá'í, I would just take the risk of making a conscious decision to be much less active, to say "no" to invitations that I did not wish to accept, and to give myself permission to define whether there were things I would really like to do for the Faith. I was aware, however, that there was a great risk of finding out that I was really a selfish spiritual slob who would never want to serve in any capacity—but even that would at least be an honest statement.

Meanwhile, since we seemed to have reached an impenetrable impasse in our marital relationship—for which, alas, I could find no solution—we decided to seek professional help, a step that would ultimately change the entire direction of my life. This, however, is not to say that I eagerly embraced the idea of going to therapy. Not much in my culture had prepared me for sharing my most intimate thoughts and feelings with a perfect stranger. I was also quite leery of the field as a whole, having heard and read about some professionals' behaviors that ranged from incompetent to unethical or immoral. I was also probably not far from a position that suggested if I had to seek professional help to resolve my marital problems, I had somehow failed as a person and, specifically, as a Bahá'í. So, essentially it was what I have come to term as the principle of "pain and panic" that brought me to therapy.

I should also say on our behalf, however, that we were committed to do whatever it took to save our marriage. We reminded ourselves of the mandate to seek out "competent physicians." Since our relationship was ailing, we agreed that we should avail ourselves of the most competent experts in the field, and we consulted at length with a Bahá'í psychologist we both loved and respected. In response to Jack's request to recommend the best therapist in the country, she suggested someone in California and a couple in Wisconsin. Since California was out of the question, we decided to concentrate on the couple based in Wisconsin. We happily discovered that they were conducting a monthly therapy group in Ozark, Missouri. Therefore, with much trepidation and some hopeful anticipation, we made the seven-hour trip to attend our first weekend-long therapy group. This was definitely the equivalent of baptism by fire.

This group consisted of about twenty people who had been meeting once a month as a group for two years. Jack had, through his work and training, been exposed to some T-groups or "sensitivity groups" in the early 1970s. I had no such exposure. It was, therefore, like walking into a world where I didn't know the rules or even the language. My attitude was a mixture of curiosity, cautiousness, and passive resistance. When one of the co-therapists referred to my attitude as "anal retentive," I remember thinking, "Lady, I don't know what you're talking about, but I'm gonna hang on to my stuff, thank you very much," not knowing that I had silently agreed with her provisional diagnosis! The group leaders were eclectic, but strongly rooted in Transactional Analysis and Gestalt therapies, and I remember being fascinated by some of the theory that was shared. The ultimate turning point in my attitude toward therapy, though, was the experiential work. It was totally magical to watch people address painful, scary, anger-provoking issues from their past or current life, and seemingly work through and resolve them.

This experience challenged some of the most fundamental beliefs about human nature, ones I had formulated with the aid of my culture and my family of origin. Statements such as "So-and-so will always be a victim of her good-heartedness" or "He was born a miser, and he is going to die a miser," coupled with a strong sense of fatalism and predeterminism, all seemed to imply that basic core-level change is not possible. The best option, in this line of thinking, was to bear one's given lot with stoic resignation and a sense of dignity. Therefore, to watch people challenge and dissect — under the expert scrutiny and guidance of the experienced therapists — messages they had been given by their parents and others about themselves, others, or the nature of life, was at once revolutionary, exciting, and bordering on blasphemy. As I watched people go through this sometimes-excruciating and sometimes-exhilarating process of discarding outmoded, dysfunctional parts of themselves, sculpting who and how they wanted to be, I felt like I had been given the privilege of witnessing the miraculous process of birth or rebirth. It was at the conclusion of one of these mesmerizing sessions, where the goal of improving our marriage appeared to be all but lost to me, that I came to the felicitous declaration in my head: "This is what I want to do when I grow up!" This spontaneous declaration felt closest to what I had heard other people state as hearing a "call" to pursue any particular path.

We soon realized that attendance at the monthly group meeting did not provide us with enough concentrated focus on our marital problems. We therefore negotiated an intensive week-long therapeutic encounter with the same co-therapists whose skills we had come to respect, and drove to Wisconsin in February 1977, leaving our five-year-old daughter with some friends. I came away from the intensive therapeutic encounter with at least two significant insights. The first was that there was hope for our marriage, and the other was that this fulfilling this hope would entail a long, difficult process that needed much patience, honesty, and hard work.

In the fall of 1977, we enrolled in a monthly training/therapy group in which some participants were learning to become therapists while others attended for personal work. For the next four years, we attended the monthly groups in Birmingham, Chattanooga, and Atlanta — always under the leadership of Dr. Josephine B. Lewis. This was the best possible training; it was a mixture of exposure to various theories of psychology, although the focus remained on Transactional Analysis and Gestalt and it was accompanied by intensive experiential work. It was an apprenticeship with a master craftsman, in which we learned by watching and doing. By 1982, I was ready to go back to college to earn a Master of Science degree in order to fulfill the State of Alabama's educational requirement to register as a psychotherapist, and graduated from Auburn University in December 1984 as a marriage and family therapist. By April 1985, I was finally, officially, in the practice of psychotherapy.

What had seemed in the mid-1970s to be a series of calamitous events aimed at destroying my emotional, psychological, and spiritual life, I now regard as crucial, divine intervention that ultimately brought me the wondrous gifts of a much more honest (and sweeter) marital life, now in its 55th year, and a most fulfilling career to which I wake up each morning with a sense of humble gratitude—but much more importantly, it brought a revolutionary change in that relationship that is ultimately the very reason for our being, my relationship with God.

In 1985, I started my private practice of psychotherapy with great excitement and anticipation. I was very fortunate to have met two very enlightened primary care physicians who recognized, accepted, and honored the interconnectedness of mental and emotional problems and their impact on physical health. At this point, I had spent many months sending out my résumé to a variety of mental health centers, without any results. The truth was that I was not at all attracted to any of these agencies; I remember that once, as I was waiting for an interview, one thought that occurred to me was "What if they offer me a job?" The feeling that accompanied this thought was one of sadness and trepidation. Of course, I badly needed a job, as I had incurred significant student loan debt, and family life had been strained by two years of commuting to graduate school at Auburn University; I had been absent a lot. At the time, my family included our two children, ages 4 and 11; Jack's daughter, Audrey, who had come to live with us at age 18; and my mother.[2] Although my husband graciously supported my decision to go back to school, in my own head I felt the pressure to start paying back, literally and figuratively. I remember that one day, disheartened by applying for these jobs that I really didn't even want, I had a spontaneous prayer that said, "You know, God, I'm really at a loss and what I need is a divine agent!" Then I laughed to myself, saying, "Yeah, right."

During my practicum at Huntingdon College, a couple had come to me for marital therapy. One day, after their session, when I briefly shared my frustration with my job-hunting, my client asked, "Why don't you work with my father?" I later found out that his father was a highly respected physician and pediatric surgeon in his 70s practicing with a Canadian doctor in his 40s. My client, who had recently returned from Canada to become his father's office manager, arranged an interview for me with these two wonderful physicians—his father, Dr. Hugh McGuire, and the younger Dr. Frank Gogan. I was immediately gratified by their enlightened

---

[2] Prior to that time, Audrey was living with her grandparents, who would not agree to have her join our family. As soon as she turned 18 years old, she came to us. Even though she was not with us for the first 18 years, we now have more than made up for that time through our close mother–daughter relationship—another one of God's blessings.

views of the inter-connectedness of mental, emotional, and physical health; they openly shared with me their awareness that many of the patients they saw really needed to see a therapist. They were very warm and respectful, and said they would welcome me as part of their practice. I was overcome by a deep sense of joyful gratitude, and mentally thanked God for hearing and responding to my prayer for a "divine agent" who had brought me to such an ideal position. Since then, I have experienced many life-changing events that I had nothing to do with, and I have learned to gratefully acknowledge and accept them as divine interventions.

The Practice of Psychotherapy:
"I Did It My Way..."

Shortly afterward I joined their practice, called "The Family Doctor," and Cameron McGuire composed a wonderful letter that they sent out to all of their patients. The letter appears here (Figure 1).

They didn't really have enough space for me to have a separate office, so I started out by seeing clients in the evenings after the physicians had left. Looking back, I see the perfection of this beginning for me. These two unique physicians had gained the total trust of their patients through their excellent rapport, so when they urged those patients to see me, they complied, even though the suggestion may not have initially made any sense to them. For most of them visiting me was their very first meeting with a therapist; in fact, some of them would say, "I don't even know why I'm here, but I trust Dr. Gogan and he said I should come see you." Soon it became apparent that I really needed more space, so the practice bought an old character-filled house just behind the Family Doctor offices, and I, along with the office manager and an accountant, moved into it. I had two lovely rooms to myself! With great enthusiasm, I painted the inside of the house, bought some attractive secondhand furniture, and created a welcoming space. Now that I had my own space during the day, these beloved doctors could, and often did, send me their patients, right after their own appointments with them. They would say, "You really need to go next door to see our counselor," or "If she is not free right now, make an appointment for later." This arrangement was truly ideal, because I got to see such an incredible array of patients ranging in age from 14 to 74, from all socioeconomic, multiracial, and ethnic backgrounds with an equally impressive array of concerns. Some were working with personality, eating, or bipolar disorders, while others were recovering from childhood sexual abuse or addressing issues as adult children of alcoholics. There were

Figure 1. Letter sent to patients of "The Family Doctor" informing them that I had joined the practice.

people who wanted to confront stress-related problems, hypertension, and smoking cessation, in addition to couples dealing with infidelity or simply hoping to enrich their relationships. It was incredibly exciting as well as intimidating for a novice therapist. Officially, I had only finished a two-year master's program in Marriage and Family Therapy, but in reality I had also had several years of amazing foundation-building and apprenticeship with Dr. Josephine Lewis. Although the work with Dr. Lewis did not bestow a license or certificate, it was priceless training that gave me great confidence in my craft.

Despite all of my preparation, some of the clients' problems left me anxious and bewildered. Luckily, I was still under the supervision of a young, innovative, and daring professor from Auburn University, so I presented him with some of my challenging cases and received guidance and much encouragement from him in exchange. In addition, my practice's clientele gradually expanded, and was no longer limited to referrals from The Family Doctor. Some friends and members of the Bahá'í community, sometimes local and sometimes very much not, were coming to see me. Since I had initially learned to do therapy as part of a group, I had experienced first-hand the advantages of this therapeutic form—so I started my first therapy group in 1988 in Birmingham, Alabama, in the home of Sonya Bennett.

This group's founding was a very significant milestone for me as a therapist. My beloved friend Sonya, who at the time I had dubbed as the "mother nurturer of the South," provided an ideal crucible for my first foray into leading a therapy group. Sonya's love and belief in the value of my work was an empowering, invaluable confirmation. Typical of her loving and generous heart, she hosted our monthly Group, of which she herself was a member, in her beautiful home on Cahaba Road. We met in her living room, which was painted a beautiful red and trimmed with white. We called this the Renoir Red Room; I think that must have been the name of the paint color. Sonya had an innate appreciation for beauty and its profound impact on the soul. Her generous, loving, nurturing hospitality, which included providing us with delicious lunches on Group days, truly fed both body and soul. She also became a self-appointed promoter of my work. I am eternally grateful for her loving, supportive presence in my life; she is truly one of a kind. Our friendship has continued and deepened through all the joys, trials, and tribulations in our respective lives, and I have come to admire and respect her sweet and stalwart soul.

From the beginning, the accepted rule of not doing therapy with friends did not make sense to me. I followed a course of experimenting with what felt right and good to both me and those who were seeking my help. As part of the intake process, I would share with clients that I regarded us as equals, instead of seeing myself as the "well person" and them as people with problems. I believed then, as I do now, that we are all on the same journey toward wholeness and authenticity, which is our birthright. As Joseph Zinker writes in his book, *In Search of Good Form*,

> In the end, we believe there is no such thing as a "therapist," only a more experienced patient....It is one thing to help someone to adjust to a situation and another to be a moving presence, a presence that stimulates spiritual transcendence rather than mere survival. In Gestalt therapy we believe that we tend to affect the couple or family through personal encounter in the moment, and more by who we are than what we do. The innate ability of the therapist to be an evocative presence comes from the horizontal and vertical depth of his or her

"apperceptive mass," the life-well of personal experience. This is why the breadth of our own personal experiences—our private therapy, our love and sorrows, travels, education, passions, and memories—is so important to us as individuals and as professionals. (291–92)

Therefore, whenever it was appropriate, I would share my own struggles, setbacks, and victories. I also attempted to inculcate in my clients a sense of pride to have sought therapy in the first place; as a result, most of my group members (as well as those in individual therapy) adopted the view of themselves as courageous people who had chosen to seek help. Therefore, most of them spoke openly and proudly about being in therapy, recommending it to others. I think it was also helpful that I shared with them that I myself had a therapist and was attempting to "walk the talk." In fact, as I look back, the comments I heard most often as positive feedback were about my willingness to share my own journey with them, in addition to my love and concern for them.

As a fifth-generation Bahá'í, I was keenly interested in bringing together the overarching divine guidance from the Bahá'í Writings with the practical methods of bringing about change, even from the earliest days of my encounter with therapy. In fact, I named my practice "Transformation." Several passages from the Writings became the source of my inspiration, such as the following: "It is incumbent upon every man of insight and understanding to strive to translate that which hath been written into reality and action" (Bahá'u'lláh, *Gleanings*, 250). I saw therapy as a mighty tool to assist us in this translation process. There were also many passages from the Guardian that were of great assistance to me from my earliest days of this journey. And, from the beginning, I was greatly energized by a desire to share whatever felt like a discovery to me with friends, family, and the Bahá'í community. In the earliest days—the late 1970s and early 1980s—when I would present notions of psychotherapy and their parallels in the Writings, I was sometimes confronted with attitudes that said that we only need the Writings, since it is all in there, and we should not confuse ourselves with other things; sometimes, people with this mindset referred to psychotherapy as "navel gazing."

One of the concepts that seemed most challenging for the Bahá'í friends was the notion of loving ourselves. On the one hand, there are many mandates in the Writings, as there are in all religious scriptures, about the absolute necessity of knowing oneself. On the other hand, the Writings are replete with passages about overcoming the self, forgetting the self, and becoming selfless. These admonitions seemed so strong in some Bahá'í friends that to even think of love of self seemed antithetical to the Writings, because, they would point out, it was love of self that had misled many a soul down the road to spiritual perdition. Bringing up the fact that the Writings mention two selves—the higher self, which is created in the image of God, and the lower self, which is the part we share with the animal kingdom (the ego that if not tamed and trained would be the cause of our downfall)—did not seem to help. Apparently, this concern and question had been brought up to 'Abdu'l-Bahá because there is this statement from Him: "Regarding the statement in The Hidden Words, that man must renounce his own self, the meaning is that he must renounce his inordinate desires, his selfish purposes and the promptings of his human self" (*Selections*, 207).

It felt like there was great fear of approaching the self, even verbally, which was very troubling to me. Although I was very excited about the tools I was discovering in psychotherapy that I found indispensable in my own journey toward self-knowledge, I could not totally dismiss the resistance I felt in others. This back-and-forth would create doubt in my findings, to the point that I would chastise myself by thinking things like, "Well, maybe you are led by your own ego!" or "What is all this passion about loving the self?" Ultimately, however, I could not let go of either the passages from the Writings about self-knowledge nor the practical psychological guidance that would be of great assistance to this process.

I received great peace and certitude by knowing that we have been created "to know and to worship God," and felt exhilaration after reading passages that seemed to equate the very purpose of our creation ("to know and to worship God") with knowing ourselves.

> *O My servants! Could ye apprehend with what wonders of My munificence and bounty I have willed to entrust your souls, ye would, of a truth, rid yourselves of attachment to all created things, and would gain a true knowledge of your own selves—a knowledge which is the same as the comprehension of Mine own Being.* (Bahá'u'lláh, *Gleanings*, 326)

This passage informed my mind and my soul that the struggle to "gain a true knowledge" of myself seems to be inextricably tied to the very reason for my creation, "to know and to worship God." Could it be any more explicit or emphatic? My resolve was further galvanized by this passage:

> *Whatever duty Thou hast prescribed unto Thy servants of extolling to the utmost Thy majesty and glory is but a token of Thy grace unto them, that they may be enabled to ascend unto the station conferred upon their own inmost being, the station of the knowledge of their own selves.* (Bahá'u'lláh, *Gleanings*, 4)

Another quick passage reads, "True loss is for him whose days have been spent in utter ignorance of his self" (Bahá'u'lláh, *Tablets of Bahá'u'lláh*, 156).

I remember in those early days, whether in my therapy groups or as a speaker at Bahá'í settings, that I would invite an individual to stand up and regard himself with true detachment, as a soul created in the image of God. Why would he not lovingly engage in knowing this self and not be fair and just to it? Sometimes I would ask the individual to apologize to his soul or higher self for not having lovingly and respectfully befriended it in the past.

By this time my passion for this topic, as well as the receptivity of many of my workshop attendants who encouraged me to "write down this stuff," inspired me to consider writing a book. In the summer of 1991, I would meet with Kim MacQueen, the beloved friend of my heart, mind, and soul, and make tentative attempts at what might be included in such a book. Writing a book, however, required another journey on my part.

Becoming an Author

In 1985, at the beginning of my practice, I had written to the Universal House of Justice (the Bahá'í governing Body of the world) to ask for prayers for spiritual and professional success on behalf of myself and my family. As I look back, I see a chain of significant events occurring in our lives subsequent to that letter. Jack was appointed as an Auxiliary Board member in 1986 (a position of service dedicated to the Faith); I was appointed to the Bahá'í National Committee of Women in 1987 and served until its dissolution in 1992. Working with this Committee was an absolute gift from God that greatly deepened my understanding of the practical applications of the principle of equality between women and men

On an even more personal level, 1986 blessed us with meeting Kim and Julian MacQueen at a District Convention; they had just returned from Canada and moved to Gulf Breeze, Florida. From then on, the lives of our respective families became totally intertwined in unforeseen and unimaginable ways—we even became officially related when our daughter, Minou, married Kim's nephew, Robert Rysiew, in 2000. Our son and Kim's daughter also shared a strong bond of friendship, and practically grew up as brother and sister. I consider my friendship with Kim a divine intervention in my life—I say divine intervention because through the close bond of our hearts and souls, we were able to create a realm of love and safety that became a sacred space for our mutual yet separate paths of spiritual transformation. There are two quotes that reflect my feelings toward our friendship. One is as follows: "Trouble is a sieve through which we sift our acquaintances. Those too big to pass through are our friends" (commonly attributed to Arlene Francis). The second is one in which 'Abdu'l-Bahá describes the bond of friendship united with the love of God:

> *The love of God has brought us together, and this is the best of means and motive. Every other bond of friendship is limited in effectiveness, but*

fellowship based upon the love of God is unlimited, everlasting, divine and radiant. (Promulgation, 442)

As I look back, I see two souls who had already endured many tests and difficulties sharing a deep thirst for exploring spiritual mysteries and an equally strong yearning for authenticity. Through Kim's loving and perceptive eyes, constant encouragement, and the safety of our friendship, I have learned to love and respect my strengths as well as my limitations. Lest one should think that our friendship consisted only of very serious topics, I should add that it has overflowed with unimaginable fun and mirth! In our encounters we have often traversed from the sublime to the ridiculous, and equally enjoyed both!

The following is an example of Kim's lovely interventions. In my email to her, I am complaining about yet another episode of Chronic Fatigue Syndrome.

I wrote:

> Hello, my dearest, how are you? I guess you are packing for the trip to Canada.
>
> I miss you already!
>
> Unfortunately, I have been having another bout with you know what! Of the past week, four days have been non-negotiable in-bed times! I am feeling annoyed and a bit sorry for myself. I am also sad that I have not done anything on my book for the past month, which makes me wonder if this will ever get done! Well, sorry for sharing doom and gloom! And of course, I am also grateful for all the good in my life!
>
> Let me know how you are, the good, the bad and the ugly!

Kim replied:

> Fafar joon joony,
>
> I'm sorry that you know what is overstaying its welcome. It's just visiting…just doesn't know when to leave!!!
>
> Don't worry though, this is not where you live or who you are. It's a damn medical condition that comes and goes and gets in the way…and then when it goes you laugh and write and cook and grow things… and you pray…and God loves you more than you will ever ever know.

AND you're allowed to be sad about this stupid thing that has no manners!!! Stupid thing.

And then as I write this I know that seeing it as stupid may help only a little bit. Some combination of submission, grit and faith is what you practice oh, so well in this spiritual trial…sometimes fiercely, always gracefully.

The book will be written.

I love you dearly and deeply.

I will try to reach you later

Kim

I chose to mention our friendship not only to account for its role in my own spiritual development, but also as a suggestion and recommendation to the reader to seek such friendship and fellowship. Spiritual transformation is a life-long and often difficult process in which we are urged to sacrifice parts of ourselves as we struggle to replace them with the potential "gems of inestimable value" placed within each of us. Having a loving, trusting soul to bear witness to our challenges and our efforts to overcome them is an absolute blessing from God that both expedites the process and makes the journey fun. This camaraderie is another reason for my love of therapy groups over the past 30+ years; members of my groups have often expressed the significance of the bonds they formed with one another and the positive roles these friendships have played in their individual paths toward wholeness and authenticity.

Back to my journey: between 1985 and 1990, I had a very joyful, stressful, and busy personal and professional life. By this time, Jack and I had also received training in multicultural consulting, and we worked as multicultural consultants through an organization called VISIONS (Vigorous InterventionS In Ongoing Natural Settings). The source of my biggest joy and delight was the seamlessness of what I was attempting to do in my own life through using what I taught in various Bahá'í Schools, my therapy groups, and my work with a variety of groups and organizations (e.g., Proctor & Gamble, various universities, church groups, and some governmental organizations). These organizations hired us as consultants to help them to identify problems within a diverse workforce and to offer tools to remedy them; these problems often stemmed from conscious or unconscious expressions of racism, sexism, classism, nationalism, and the like. My work as a consultant helped deepen my awareness of the harmony between science and religion: these organizations, without awareness of the healing message of the Bahá'í Faith (i.e., elimination of all forms of prejudice, equality between men and women, a world-embracing vision of humanity), were struggling with and inadvertently moving toward solutions offered by Bahá'u'lláh over a century and a half ago. As a member of the Bahá'í National Committee of Women, I had the honor and privilege to present a workshop in 1990 in Beijing, China on internalized oppression in women within Chinese culture. We learned through informal conversations with women, for example, that many couples were choosing to abort undesirable female embryos in favor of a male fetus in response to the government's one-child policy.

Inspired and motivated by my participation in these activities, as well as feedback from workshop participants asking, "Why don't you write this stuff down?", I started to think about writing a book, and in 1991, with Kim's encouragement and collaboration, we began the outline for this book. Our daughter Minou was doing a youth year of service in Haifa at the time; then, the policy was that the immediate family of youth serving in the Holy Land could visit Haifa for a week. In the summer of that year, at the end of Minou's term of service, Jack and I and our 12-year-old son had the privilege of going to the Holy Land.

During our week in Haifa, brimming with the excitement of writing such a book, I asked to meet with Dr. Peter Khan, by then a member of the Universal House of Justice. We had met the Khans at various Southeastern Bahá'í Schools (regional gatherings of Bahá'ís for the study, deepening, and fellowship of the Teachings for Bahá'ís and interested friends) when they lived in the United States. In his office at the Seat of the Universal House of Justice, I shared my ideas about writing such a book with Dr. Khan. He was very kind and encouraging, and asked me to explain some of the concepts I hoped to include. At the end of this delightful meeting, Dr. Khan prompted me to come up with an outline and submit it to the House of Justice for their perusal. I had never anticipated such a suggestion prior to the meeting. I was filled with a mixture of unutterable joy, excitement, and dread. I remember that my family and I were coming down the steps from Golomb Street to Hillel Street, I broke into a spontaneous dance as I gave them the account of my meeting. I am eternally grateful to Dr. Khan for his loving support, without which I would have never had the courage or even the thought of presenting my ideas to that august Institution.

I spent the next few months, still brimming with awe, joy, and disbelief, consolidating my ideas and putting them into outline form. Finally, by December 1991, I was ready to mail my letter. I had to mentally and spiritually prepare myself for accepting any response—hopefully, with "radiant acquiescence."

The next page is a copy of my letter to the Universal House of Justice (Figure 2); my project goals as stated in the letter are as follows.

Project Goals

- To invite the reader to awaken to him/herself with joy and curiosity, stressing that ignorance of the "self" does not constitute humility or "selflessness." The self cannot be known without a loving, attentive attitude.

- To confront a dichotomous attitude, found among some Bahá'ís, which seems to say, "If you're a good Bahá'í, you should not need anything but the Writings." This attitude keeps these friends from getting professional help when it is needed and is often contrary to the spirit of the principle of harmony between science and religion.

- To establish that personal transformation is continuous and often difficult, and to offer specific knowledge and tools to facilitate this process.

- To facilitate and legitimize others' struggles, especially fourth- and fifth-generation Bahá'ís who may feel confused or guilty about having doubts or personal problems, by sharing my own struggles as a fifth-generation Bahá'í.

- To respond to requests from Bahá'ís, with whom I have shared some of these concepts in various talks and workshops over the past ten years, and to write these concepts down so that other Bahá'í communities could have access to them.

In less than a month I received their response (Figure 3, next page).

It is difficult to describe the awe, joy, exhilaration, honor, deepest gratitude, and confirmation I felt in response to their letter. Re-reading the letter 25 years later, I am still filled with all those feelings. I also marvel at how a speck like me dared write that letter and proposal to the Universal House of Justice and be honored by their encouraging response. I then wrote the first chapter in 1992.

How can I describe the impact of the response from the Universal House of Justice on my mind and soul? In the deepest sense I felt heard, confirmed, and validated. From then on, the response from the Universal House of Justice became the firm ground on which I stood. It consolidated

𝓕arzaneh 𝒢uillebeaux
𝓜ontgomery, 𝒜labama

December 29, 1991

Universal House of Justice
Post Office Box 155
Haifa, Israel 31001

Beloved Universal House of Justice,

    In 1985 I wrote and asked for your prayers for spiritual and professional success on behalf of myself and my family. Since then, so many different doors have opened which have enabled us to serve our beloved Faith in up to then undreamt of capacities. Now once again I feel that I am at a new juncture in my spiritual and professional life. Above all I feel a sense of exhilaration, excitement and gratitude and a desire to serve the Faith in a unique way which would offer my professional skills to the threshold of Bahá'u'lláh.

    Specifically I am asking for your prayers concerning a project which is very close to my heart. I have embarked on writing a book which would bring together the Bahá'í Writings and some of the relevant and practical concepts of psychotherapy. This is not meant to be a theoretical work, but a practical handbook which I hope would be of assistance to individual believers in their process of personal transformation. Enclosed you will find more specific information about the book.

    I am requesting your prayers for the removal of all barriers, real and imagined, to this undertaking. Some of the challenges are:

- maintaining a healthy balance between making a living, attending to home and family, and rendering Bahá'í service on local, regional and national levels. For instance I have wondered if I should resign from the Bahá'í National Committee on Women, though the past five years on that committee have constituted some of my most joyful and productive Bahá'í experiences.
- feelings of inadequacy to the task.
- discounting the validity of the task.

    Please know of my deep sense of gratitude, awe and wonder for the mighty institution of the Universal House of Justice which, through its display of love, guidance and responsiveness to the cry of the individual believer, has once again emboldened me to take up some of its precious time.

Sincerely,

Farzaneh (Farfar) Guillebeaux

Enclosure

Figure 2. My letter informing the Universal House of Justice of my intention to write a book and asking for prayers for this endeavor.

THE UNIVERSAL HOUSE OF JUSTICE

BAHÁ'Í WORLD CENTRE

Department of the Secretariat   22 January 1992

Mrs. Farzaneh Guillebeaux
Montgomery, AL 36101
U.S.A.

Dear Bahá'í Friend,

Your letter of 29 December 1991, explaining your plan for a book which would bring together the Bahá'í Writings and practical aspects of psychotherapy, has been received by the Universal House of Justice which feels that your project is timely and could fill an important need in assisting the friends as they struggle with the process of spiritual transformation.

Be assured of the loving prayers of the House of Justice in the Holy Shrines that your proposed undertaking may be crowned with success.

With loving Bahá'í greetings,

For Department of the Secretariat

Figure 3. Letter from the Universal House of Justice in response to my letter.

my resolve to devote my time and energies in manifold aspects of my life to this mandate from Bahá'u'lláh: "It is incumbent upon every man of insight and understanding to strive to translate that which hath been written into reality and action" (*Gleanings*, 256).

So, why has it taken me 25 years to carry out my proposed undertaking? This is a question I have asked myself periodically. The simplest and perhaps most superficial answer is that the events of my life interfered, and that given all the givens, there was not enough time or energy to write a book. This assessment was true enough.

In retrospect, I think that I was also overwhelmed by the daunting task ahead: "Oh my God! Now that I got it, what do I do with it?" Well, what I did with it was to share it, in part and when appropriate, in Bahá'í Schools whenever reservations were expressed in the form of a false dichotomy as to whether one should spend time, energy, affection, and patience with oneself, or whether one should channel all their energies outwardly toward teaching the Cause. Often, sharing the Outline and the House's response were enough to address and alleviate their qualms. I was ever so grateful for having gotten that far with the project! Of course, the immediate question arising from the participants was then, "Well, have you written the book yet?" My response was always, "No, but I am in process." Sometimes my Critical Parent would raise its voice and attempt to shame me into writing; thank God that by then, I knew enough about myself to know that shame and guilt were very poor motivators for me! In fact, shame and guilt had the absolute opposite effect; they would drain me of all energy and motivation.

Naturally, there were ups and downs—tests and difficulties—in the intervening years. When our daughter, Minou, was diagnosed with cancer in 1995, all our attention and energies for the next two years focused on her treatments and recovery. Later, our son went through his own (as we know, our tests are quite customized) set of trials and difficulties, which again consumed much of my energies. There was also loss concerning my health and career, which I will explain in the coming pages.

From time to time, I would check in with myself and ask what was going on—why was I not writing the book? It was equally true that there seemed to be both inward and outward processes that were taking place as a result of receiving the confirming and permission-giving letter.

At the inner level, I felt a level of certitude that I had lacked before. The response from the Universal House of Justice was truly the spiritual diploma, license, or certificate I needed to carry on this work. When rereading my letter to the House of Justice, I see that I had asked for its prayers for the removal of external as well as internal barriers to the project.

The external barriers got resolved gradually (i.e., the kids growing up and moving away, etc.), but I think the elapse of these years was necessary for the removal of internal barriers: "Ultimately all the battles of life are within the individual" (Shoghi Effendi, *Directives from the Guardian*, 78). Certain important events and milestones—in the form of tests and difficulties—had to occur to deepen my level of certitude about how the spiritual or therapeutic principles would play out in my own life.

In 1991, although my intellect, heart, and soul were deeply excited and committed to the notion of bringing Bahá'í principles together with therapeutic concepts to offer tools for spiritual transformation, it would take major tests and difficulties for me to experience first-hand how this process of spiritual transformation worked. As time passed, I became able to understand that if my book largely transmitted untested spiritual or therapeutic knowledge, it might have been useful and perhaps well received by others' minds and intellects—but it would lack the necessary steps for actualization. I found a phrase from 'Abdu'l-Bahá to be illuminating: "The intellect is good, but unless it has become the servant to the heart it is of little avail" (Honnold, *Vignettes from the Life of 'Abdu'l-Bahá*, 35).

I came to appreciate the vital role of tests and difficulties in rendering the intellect a servant of the heart; I talk more about this role in Part IV. This process of integrating these spiritual and therapeutic guiding principles became more complete with my first-hand experience in applying them to my life, which allowed my comprehension at the cellular level, which in turn prepared me to be able to share them authentically with others as my truths. Otherwise, they were just good ideas.

My take-away from these reflections is that the intervening years were necessary for me to internalize the concepts and notions that I wanted to present in the book. Through the events of my life, my tests and difficulties, I was given the opportunity for first-hand experience of how various concepts, be they from the Writings or from psychotherapy, worked in real day-to-day life. This experience was heightened when I worked with others (in the context of individual, couples, and group therapy) and had the privilege of seeing the effectiveness of these principles in action in their lives as well.

As to the specific areas in my letter for which I had asked the prayers of the Universal House of Justice, their resolution was a prolonged, evolutionary process:

- To emphasize the maintenance of a healthy balance between making a living, tending to home and family, and rendering Bahá'í service, there have sometimes been very explicit events leading to the removal of a particular concern. For instance, the

- restructuring of all National Committees led to the National Spiritual Assembly's dissolution of the Committee on Women in 1992.
- In other areas, such as making a living, the developments were more implicit and gradual; only in retrospect can I recognize that they were slowly moving me toward a deeper level of prioritizing the expenditure of my energies (more about this later).
- The feelings of an "inadequacy to the task" have been the most prolonged struggle, even to this very moment. Up to a point, there is definitely truth in this stance, maybe even a universal one; I think it is healthy for us to be in touch with our own impotence in any spiritual endeavor. However, this feeling of impotence and inadequacy can easily and equally be the pathological manifestation of a particular "prison of self" (see Part III, "Okay Corral"). So, a great part of the internal struggle has been bringing myself out of the debilitating dark features of my own "prison of self" into the empowering bright light of what God wants for us all. To the part of me that would say something like "Look at you, it is pitiful that you are still dealing with this issue, or these issues," the Guardian's statement seemed to legitimize my internal battles. Rather than seeing myself as wasting time with my struggles, I could elevate them to the worthy goal of "fighting my own spiritual battles" and making progress "little by little, day by day" ('Abdu'l-Bahá, in *The Bahá'í World Vol. 12*, 706).

It was these two-plus decades, with their many joys, sorrows, tests, and trials, that helped me deepen my own understanding of both the Guidance of the Writings and the significance of sound therapeutic tools in fighting my own spiritual battles.

In one sense, I received and interpreted the answer to my prayer regarding my sense of inadequacy to the task as a paradox: "Yes, Fafar, you will always be inadequate to the task, and on the other hand, you will be provided with life situations to help you develop more adequacy ☺. Then you will hopefully be able to both embrace and get over your feeling of inadequacy—and go ahead with doing the task anyhow."

- As to the third area of questioning, the "validity of the task," after receiving the answer from the House of Justice, I no longer questioned it. As I have said before, its response became the solid foundation on which I stood. This whole experience has also taught me that yes, indeed, God hears and answers all prayers;

however, that answer can be protracted through many, many years. I needed to be receptive, alert, and patient in order to recognize, receive, and digest the answers.

More than two decades later, I am ready to share my understanding and my application of that understanding in my life with you—not as a model for emulation, but as a model of someone who has been passionate about living consciously and knitting together the overarching guidance of the Bahá'í Writings with the practical, nascent social science tools in service of my own spiritual growth and my journey toward wholeness and authenticity. In Part II, I share some of the language and theory that was crucial to my own journey, as well as to my ability to assist others in theirs, with the aim of translating "that which has been written into reality and action" (Bahá'u'lláh, *Gleanings*, 250).

Part II
Some Theoretical Foundations for Spiritual Transformation

In Part II, I lay the groundwork for spiritual transformation, beginning with a quick introduction to the Three Basic Questions, which may help you get to know yourself a little better by interrogating your own narrative. I then explore a few ways in which change can happen. The following concepts are ones that I found very useful in my own journey.

The Three Basic Questions

Below, I discuss some of the Transactional Analysis principles that were very helpful in my process of getting to know myself. The first one is the notion that we come into the world feeling okay about ourselves and others; we know this notion to be true because a newborn baby is totally vulnerable even as she is well-equipped to let us know her needs, which implies an innate trust that she will be tended to and her needs will be met.

The second notion is that we, as people, appear to be born with a mandate to survive. In order to achieve this mandate, though, we need answers to these basic questions:

1. "Who am I?"
2. "Who are the others?"
3. "How will I make it?"

A baby starts to engage with these intrinsic survival questions at a very basic level. The first few months of life he continues his symbiotic relationship initiated in the womb with his mother; however, the infant gains gradual awareness of himself as a being separate from his mother, answering the "Who am I?" question. A provisional answer to the first question is something like, "I am an entity apart and separate from mother." Once the self is experienced as separate from the mother, it progresses to the second question: "Who are the others?" This question is at first answered by the role the mother or caretaker plays (i.e., this "other" feeds me, protects me, plays with me, etc.) — so, the "others" seem to be okay as well, which reinforces the first notion.

We enter the world keenly interested in forming answers to the third question, "How will I make it?" The innate programming for survival is suggested by the infants' self-centeredness; they make their needs known by crying when hungry, wet, hurting, or wanting contact. The primitive answer to this question is, "Wow, I badly need this mother (caretaker) person around for my survival."

This deep need to find answers to these three questions remains with us for the rest of our earthly lives, but during the first five years of life, we are busily engaged in answering these questions. Two sets of features seem to impact a child's responses: one is the individual child's intrinsic characteristics, and the other is comprised of the conditions into which the child is born (e.g., the parents' own physical and mental health, their socio-economic status, whether there are other siblings, the infant's gender placement, etc.). In those first crucial years, the child forms provisional answers to these questions — and these answers will affect all of their future decisions. With this in mind, we can see how important it is to make the effort to become aware of our answers to these critical questions! These answers need to be identified so that, if necessary, they may be challenged or reshaped to be healthy guides for our future choices.

In Transactional Analysis theory, we sometimes refer to these provisional answers to the Three Basic Questions as "early decisions." This turn of phrase does not mean that the child sits somewhere on a fine day and makes these decisions; it is an organic, spontaneous, and gradual process based on the child's constant, continuous observations and absorption, and the conclusions she draws from them about the self and the others. By the time we reach adulthood, we are totally unaware that these were our conclusions based on a specific set of circumstances; for the most part, we accept those conclusions as our absolute reality. That, however, is akin to building a house on quicksand.

As I think about what my own answers to the Three Basic Questions may have been at age 5, I come up with the following:

1. I am bright, cute, and lovable; tricky and selfish; and worthy of praise and attention.
2. Others love me sometimes just as I am — but mostly when I do things that please them.
3. In order to survive I have to look my best, and vigilantly observe others in order to figure out what I need to do to please them or trick them into loving me, and into giving me attention and affection.

Of course, the answers to these questions vary greatly from person to person. A child who is mistreated, neglected, and abused, verbally or physically, may have these answers:

1. I am ugly, unlovable, not worthy, and so forth.
2. Others are cruel, selfish, temperamental, dangerous, untrustworthy, and unpredictable.
3. I must be and act the way in which they define me; I can't trust or get close to others.

You can imagine all the possible variations of these answers. I encourage you to discover your own set of provisional answers and early decisions about yourself and others. Some readers may have come up with their own answers through therapy, reading self-help books, or by reading the Writings. For others this experience may be a new one, and they may find it challenging or even scary. If you have difficulty coming up with what your initial answers may have been, you could sit in a quiet place where you won't be disturbed, close your eyes, and go back to as many early scenes—preferably from five years old or younger—of your childhood as you can. In your mind's eye, try to see yourself interacting with others. With some concentration and a lot of practice, you can even come up with what you were feeling (glad, mad, sad, scared) and/or thinking.

Another element that can help you in this quest is how you have been treated, either currently or throughout your life. For the most part, people treat us according to how we have inwardly defined ourselves and them (i.e., if my experience is that I am often treated without respect, chances are I suffer from low self-esteem; hence, I don't believe that I deserve others' respect).

I believe that in order to fulfill the mandate of knowing ourselves—"Man should know his own self and recognize that which leadeth unto loftiness or lowliness, glory or abasement, wealth or poverty" (Bahá'u'lláh, *Tablets of Bahá'u'lláh*, 34)—it is absolutely necessary for each individual to come up with truthful answers to the Three Basic Questions. If we assume that our goal in life is to grow and develop spiritually, we first have to make an honest assessment of where we are before we set out to change anything.

Options for Making Change Happen

My first trainer in Transactional Analysis used to say that three things can challenge our provisional image of self and others:

1. Falling in love,
2. therapy, and
3. divine intervention (such as conversion to a religion, both in terms of what God has revealed throughout the ages through His Messengers and Prophets, and miraculous events that can change the course of a life. The latter is often a result of a close encounter with death, be it an accident or a terminal diagnosis).

Let's look at the efficacy of these three options. In the first one (falling in love), seeing ourselves through the eyes of one who loves us is euphoric, magical, and potentially healing. There is tremendous power when negative notions about oneself are lovingly challenged by a person we love and trust. For a person who may have a healthy and positive self-image, these self-conceptions can be affirmed and confirmed in a loving relationship. I believe that this experience, like the goal of procreation, is also a primary goal of the divine institution of marriage: "the institution of marriage as conceived and established by Bahá'u'lláh, is…of a vital social importance, constituting as it does the very foundation of social life" (from a letter written on behalf of Shoghi Effendi, in Hornby, *Lights of Guidance*, 377).

> *And when He desired to manifest grace and beneficence to men, and to set the world in order, He revealed observances and created laws; among them He established the law of marriage, made it as a fortress for well-being and salvation, and enjoined it upon us in that which was sent down out of the heaven of sanctity in His Most Holy Book.* (Bahá'í prayer for marriage by Bahá'u'lláh, in *Bahá'í Prayers*, 116)

In fact, spouses are enjoined to be concerned with not just each other's physical wellbeing, but also their spiritual wellbeing. If each partner enters the union committed to following the above-mentioned guidance, marriage can become the perfect crucible for each individual's growth and development.

> *The true marriage of Bahá'ís is this, that husband and wife should be united both physically and spiritually, that they may ever improve the spiritual life of each other, and may enjoy everlasting unity throughout all the worlds of God.* ('Abdu'l-Bahá, *Selections*, 118)

However, falling in love also has its limitations. If I base my definition of myself primarily on how someone else sees me, I am giving them more power than they should have, and I am too dependent on their opinion. Suppose there is a rupture in the relationship, and I am no longer seen as wonderful and lovable—there goes my newly established positive self-image. It is likely that the ever-present negative noise in my head will say something like "Well, as we've always known, you're really unlovable, unworthy" or "You have believed you were lovable and now you have been proven wrong!" I believe that our Creator wants each individual to know and to value him- or herself independently of others' opinions. As I mentioned earlier, my own sense of self-worth was highly threatened when Jack expressed his dissatisfaction toward our union; I saw myself as an "utter failure!"

The second option is seeking therapy, which can be a powerful route to personal empowerment. Selected carefully, a skilled therapist can give us a third eye through which we can objectively examine and challenge our well-established (albeit on a foundation of sand) beliefs about self and others, as well as our roadmap charting our life's course. Obviously, choosing a skilled and trustworthy therapist is of the utmost importance. If done correctly, not only will my perceptions of myself, others, and my life plan be scrutinized and challenged, but I will be given tools to work with that will allow me to choose consciously who and how I want to be, and what role I want others to play in my life. Productive and effective therapy empowers an individual to be responsive rather than reactive to life events.

One drawback to the therapeutic approach can occur when one adopts an attitude that someone other than themselves can "fix me and my life." People who have sought therapy with this attitude might make comments, such as "I tried counseling, but it didn't help or it is not for me." This comment and ones like it can be caused by choosing the wrong therapist, or by not engaging seriously in the process, or by believing that the therapist can and should "fix" the problems with minimal effort on the part of the client. But even in the process of therapy, one should not let go of being in charge of one's overall wellbeing. Ideally, it should be a process where at the beginning the therapist plays a much more active role, with the goal that over time, more and more power and responsibility will be shifted to the client. I believe that at the beginning of the therapeutic process dependence on the therapist is appropriate and okay, as long as both the therapist and the client understand and agree that it is a temporary dependence and that they are both mutually and explicitly moving toward decreasing this dependency and working toward the ultimate goal of autonomy.

My own experience with my beloved and brilliant therapist, the late Dr. Josephine Lewis, followed this pattern. At the beginning of our therapeutic encounter, I felt that I could not live my life without her input and I felt quite dependent on her. I think I voiced my concern about the level of my dependence, and I am sure that she reassured me that it was a temporary phase. During this initial phase of therapy, I felt powerless, sad, and confused. My own image of my life was that I lived under overcast skies, and the glimmers of hope I gained after my sessions with Jo were like the sun poking its head through the gloom. At first these breakthroughs were quite temporary, and back I would go to my gray skies. Gradually, and initially without my conscious awareness, this ratio began to change, until one day, returning from a therapy session, I burst out laughing in the realization that most of my days were now sunny with an occasional overcast day!

The third and potentially most powerful change-producing component is that of divine intervention. Here the reality is that we have been created by a loving God, Who has given us a soul that is potentially capable of reflecting all the qualities and attributes of God, and Who has provided a clear definition of who we are and the purpose of this earthly life. There are several pitfalls in this component as well, however: (1) I may not believe that there is a God, or if there is one that He is not intimately concerned with my life; (2) I may believe He's there and cares about me, but I don't take the time to study and deepen my knowledge of what He has said about Himself, me, and the desired relationship between us; and (3) I may not understand that even though He has provided the perfect plan, it is my responsibility to read it, understand it, and then put it into action. "All that which ye potentially possess can be manifested only as a result of your own volition" (Bahá'u'lláh, *Gleanings*, 149). It can also be the case, as it was in my experience, that the guidance seems too lofty, at times seemingly vague, paradoxical, and impossible to achieve—so why bother?

For me, personally, the discovery of therapy—through the impetus of pain and panic described in the first chapter—gave me the necessary alphabet and the means "to strive to translate that which hath been written into reality and action" (Bahá'u'lláh, *Gleanings*, 250). Therefore, as I look back, I now see the loving and firm divine intervention that violently shook the ground on which I was standing—my fragile sense of self-acceptance and wellbeing based on my husband's love for me. So, this disruption pushed me to seek therapy, the second component of change. Therapy challenged many of my notions of who I was, who were the others, and how to make it in this life.

It was through the process of therapy, as well as continued divine interventions—often in the form of severe tests and difficulties—that I was able to get a much clearer understanding of the third component of change. Obviously, I am not suggesting that this should be the path of spiritual transformation for everyone; I am simply saying this is how it happened in my life and relaying the lessons I learned along the way.

Through experimenting in my own life, I experienced the truth of the necessity for science and religion to work hand-in-hand. For me, the overarching guidance of the Faith was at once too lofty, unreachable, and therefore, overwhelming at times, leaving me bereft, defeated, and powerless. On the other hand, applying science (here, the nascent field of psychology) without the illuminating guidance of my Creator's definition of who I am and why I was created in the first place was lame, limited, and limiting! It was truly the unity of science and religion that brought balance to my life and allowed me to employ both.

Getting to Know Me through Ego States

> My business is not to remake myself,
> but make the absolute best of what God made.
> —Robert Browning (in Scudder, *The Complete Poetic and Dramatic Works*, 352)

One of the first concepts that helped start my process of gaining self-knowledge was put forth by Eric Berne, the founder of Transactional Analysis (TA). Once again, I am not promoting any particular theory, nor am I attempting to give a full explanation of the theory I share; for that, I refer the reader to see the recommended readings at the end of this book which I hope will whet your appetite and rouse your curiosity for learning more about TA. My goal in this chapter is to share what helped me in my processes, and what in turn I have used to help others.

This particular concept divides the "self" into three components called "ego states" (Figure 4):

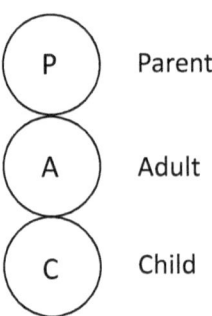

Figure 4. Structural diagram of ego states.

The parent ego state contains all that we were taught by our parents, or our caregivers, relatives, schools, religious training, and our culture at large. This ego state contains the notions of right, wrong, and all of the "how-tos" that were introduced to us from various external sources; it is the sum total of all that we were taught. In other words, it is the totality of what each individual has internalized from their own parents and caregivers. The language of this ego state is "parental," so it contains a lot of "shoulds," "musts," and "have-tos."

The adult ego state is the part that is in touch with "here and now" reality. It observes and reports data.

The child ego state is the storehouse of all our feelings; it is self-centered, energetic, creative, fun-loving, and full of life. It does not like responsibility. My trainer-mentor, Dr. Josephine Lewis, used to say that four-fifths of each person's energy is stored in the child ego state. The theory also divides the ego states according to the roles and functions they play within the personality. The following diagram displays the various functions of each ego state (Figure 5).

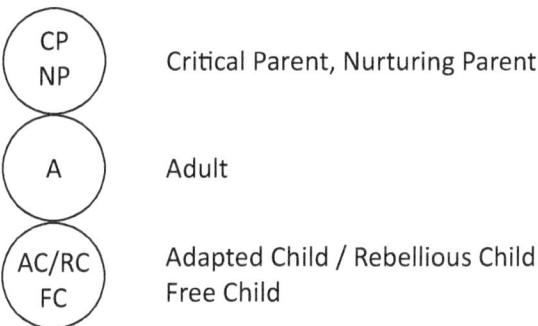

Figure 5. Functional diagram of ego states, or Parent/Adult/Child (PAC) circles.

The Critical (also referred to as Controlling) Parent has the function of establishing boundaries, giving us all the "dos" and "don'ts," teaching us right and wrong, and so on. Nurturing Parent is the part that loves us unconditionally—"I love you because you are"—whereas Critical Parent's love is more conditional: "I love you when you do right, or when you do what I want you to do." The Nurturing Parent role can become overly permissive; however, the term Critical Parent does not connote negativity. Its function is to provide vital guidance that allows us to develop our individual conscience by teaching us cause and effect, and setting necessary limits to our behaviors. Ideally, there should be a balance between the critical and nurturing functions; too much of either one is as detrimental as not enough.

The function of the adult ego state is to serve as the executive of the personality. When functioning correctly, it will mediate between the demands and mandates of the parent ego state and the wishes and whims of the child ego state; helping them come to a compromise that is agreeable to both. In short, the Adult is the problem solver—when working properly, it anchors the person in reality and diffuses ongoing battles between Parent and Child.

The child ego state is divided into two basic functions, Free Child and Adapted Child. The Free Child is the part we are born with. It engages in magical thinking. Its orientation is all or nothing, and it does not like responsibility. The Adapted Child can be the obedient, compliant part of the Child that adapts to the counsels and demands given by the parent ego state. The Adapted Child can also manifest itself in passive or active rebellion, sometimes referred to as the Rebellious Child. Balance is needed between Free Child, Adapted Child, and, when necessary, Rebellious Child, just as it is between Critical and Nurturing Parent.

Now, I'll attempt to acquaint you with some of the contents of my ego states. First, I present the contents pre-therapy, and later I share how the contents have been modified. To say that my parent ego state was definitely out of balance is an understatement! My Critical Parent definitely dominated my Nurturing Parent; there were multitudes of expectations and demands. Given that I was a fifth-generation Bahá'í, with a well-known and respected Bahá'í ancestry, it is not surprising that the "acquiring of perfections" was expected and treated as a divine mandate. So, the dominance of these expectations resulted in conditional love: I was good and worthy of affection as long as (and to the degree that) I met those qualification and expectations. My Adult, when on the job, was strong in its capacity for observing data and drawing appropriate conclusions, but not strong enough to intervene between my top-heavy Parent and emaciated Child.

As a direct response to the imbalance in my parent ego state, my child ego state was also out of balance in that I had a very dominant and overdeveloped Adapted Child, a "terminal good-girl syndrome," and very little Free Child. Part of the Adapted Child's manifestation, however, was a heavy dose of passive rebellion. So, as a whole person, I was totally "duty" bound, constantly forcing myself to follow many "shoulds" and often feeling guilty because I felt that I was failing. Because my Free Child and (for the most part) my adult ego states were missing in action, I carried out my duties rather lifelessly. At the time of my momentary paralysis described in the first chapter, I was at the apex of the above description; outwardly active and engaged in doing all the right things, but inwardly empty, alone, confused and depressed.

In Transactional Analysis practice, the measurement of these various functions is expressed in the form of an "egogram" (see Dusay, *Egograms*). My egogram pre-therapy would have looked something like Figure 6.

The contents of the parent and child ego states are, for the most part, what we swallowed whole as it was given to us, primarily, by our parents or caregivers. I say, "swallowed whole" because for those first few years, which are so crucial to the formation of our self-concept and self-identity, we are totally at the mercy of our parents. That reality is why all the world's scriptures put such emphasis on the importance of parental duties for the education and training of children.

The Bahá'í Writings compare the child to a young sapling that is at first pliable and malleable, but the older the tree becomes the harder it is to shape. What we as parents have not quite internalized is the fact that children are like the keenest scientists at work: they observe and absorb, sponge-like, all that is going on around them. In this respect, they are far

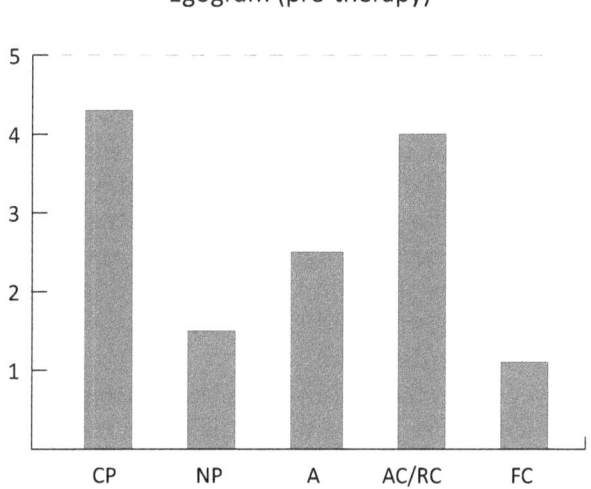

Figure 6. CP = Critical Parent; NP = Nurturing Parent; A = Adult; AC/RC = Adapted Child/Rebellious Child; FC = Free Child. Adapted from *Egograms: How I See You and You See Me*, by Jack Dusay (1977).

more affected by what they see us do, rather than what we say—giving credence to the phrase "more is caught than taught."

This developmental reality is incredibly exciting to me, in that as a person focuses on their own spiritual development, their own being has the greatest impact on the health and wellbeing of their offspring. Since the fetus is sustained and nurtured by the mother from its very beginning, our understanding and appreciation of the role of mother as the first trainer is also deepened. Most schools of psychology, however, agree that the foundation of a child's personality is laid during the child's first five years. Thus, by the ripe old age of five, we have provisional answers to the Three Basic Questions: Who am I? Who are the others? How will I make it?

Although the first five years are critical in childhood development, there is no such thing as perfect parents or parenting; there is, of course, a wide-ranging spectrum on which parents (and parenting) fall. Parents may be economically stable or poverty stricken, educated or ignorant; similarly, their parenting style may be loving or unkind, responsible or irresponsible. Most fall somewhere in between the extremes. The fact is that since there is no such thing as perfect parents and parenting, each person's answers to the Three Basic Questions contain some misinformation, even in the best-case scenario, until they are confronted, updated, and corrected.

It should also be noted that not only do we form our definition of self, others, and a life-sustaining plan during these first five years, we also form our very first notions of a Creator. In fact, since as children we have no power and the grown-ups are in total control (or so it seems), we see these adults as God figures. Once again, who and how they are is as important as how and whether they talk to us about God. So, if we were to add a fourth and fifth question to the Three Basic Questions, they would be "Who is God?" and "What role if any does He play in my life?" When asked to appraise, identify, and evaluate their parents' treatment of them, most clients in therapy become highly protective and want to state that "they were really good people and I know they did the best they could." At this point, the therapist should point out that the parents are not on trial; we are not here to judge them.

In fact, I have often pointed out to a client during a session that just by the fact that they were sitting there talking to me, I knew that they received a lot of unconditional love, such as when they were fed and cared for as babies, as well as lots of conditional love, which enabled them to function in the world. The point here is that everyone who wants to grow and develop spiritually needs to identify what they swallowed whole, so that they can unearth any misinformation about themselves. To me, this investigation represents becoming an adult and taking full responsibility for who I am and how I want to be. So, the therapist's process of gathering information about their parents and their input is the equivalent of a physician ordering blood tests or x-rays; it is a fact-finding activity, not one of judgment or backbiting. In fact, in this process the individual can also gain a deeper appreciation for all that their parents did well.

Here, I refer to two passages from the Writings that I find applicable. One is "the independent investigation of truth" ('Abdu'l-Bahá, *Selections*, 248). I know that normally we refer to it in the area of one's chosen religious pathway and that it warns us against blind imitation of our parents, culture, and so on. This phrase also alerts us to the fact that it is each soul's privilege and responsibility to "independently investigate" truth, which implies a conscious, objective search for truth, which in turns leads one to the subjectively chosen personal path.

Obviously, the principle of "the independent investigation of truth" does not have to be limited to religious truth! I believe that we are guided to use our God-given faculties to study and discover "truth" in any of life's arenas. For me, this notion is further affirmed through this Writing from Bahá'u'lláh:

O Son of Spirit!

The best beloved of all things in My sight is justice; turn not away therefrom if thou desirest Me, and neglect it not that I may confide in thee. By its aid thou shalt see with thine own eyes and not through the eyes of others, and shalt know of thine own knowledge and not through the knowledge of thy neighbor. Ponder this in thy heart; how it behooveth thee to be. Verily justice is My gift to thee and a sign of My loving-kindness. Set it then before thine eyes. (*Hidden Words*, 3)

The Creative Word has more meanings and applications than we will ever know. As a therapist attempting to find harmony between the Writings and helpful psychotherapeutic concepts, I was thrilled and exhilarated when I connected the possible application of the above Hidden Word to the process of knowing the "self." If my notion of who I am is largely based on how two other human beings—themselves far from perfect— saw and defined me, and I absorbed it as absolute truth, wouldn't it make sense that I should now, as an adult, attempt to see and get to know myself through my own eyes, and then decide how I want to improve? I could understand that this self-knowledge would be a divine "gift" and a sign of His loving kindness.

I saw plenty of evidence of the ways in which various clients had internalized attributions made by their parents and caregivers as their absolute reality. I will share a few examples of how these distortions can manifest in a person's life if they are not confronted and corrected:

1. As hypochondria, if parental attention mostly came when the child was sick or not doing well. A child could develop the habit of putting himself in trouble's way to create a trauma, because part of him believes it will bring the necessary attention and affection.

2. As a belief of being dumb (or below average intelligence), and only finding out later in life that they had an above-average IQ, leading to shock.

3. A message of "stay daddy's or mommy's little girl" might be internalized into "don't grow to become a fully developed woman," and become the root of some clients' suffering with eating disorders.

4. As a resolution (or conclusion), based on early experience, that the person becomes worthy of affection and attention only after they have taken care of everybody else's needs and wants.

Now, let's say that I decide to see myself through my own eyes, and conduct an independent investigation of who I am. My own self-assessment will be inadequate if I do not go to the Source and explore who my Creator says I am. I sometimes call this process "referring to the Owner's Manual." Although I go into more detail about this process later, let me summarize it here: if you buy a vehicle—really, any machine—and want to get the optimum service out of it, you need to read and study the manual that spells out the manufacturer's guidance and recommendations (i.e., what will prolong or shorten its life, what it can and cannot do, etc.). If you remain unfamiliar with the "Owner's Manual" content, you will go through a lot of trial and error—mostly error in my case—and you may end up paying a heavy price for your ignorance. In my frustration with this process, I might lay blame on the manufacturer or others, and refuse to take responsibility for my part of the problem. I know that many of us, myself included, are resistant to reading instructions (e.g., the Owner's Manual) until there is a problem, which may then send me to do what I should have done from the beginning, only now in a fit of despair or frustration. This behavior could be analogous to the pain and panic that urges us to go to the Writings, or pray, or seek therapy.

The above example may be superficial; like all analogies, it has its limitations. However, I think it could be helpfully applied to the process of gaining self-knowledge. For instance, the latest Revelation from God reaffirms what has been said in all Scriptures by defining me primarily as a spiritual being in a physical body for a hundred or so years, at most. The implication of just this one fact is so far-reaching that whole books could be written about it. How much or how well I struggle with understanding and accepting my spiritual reality informs my major decisions, my reactions and responses to the inevitable difficulties I face, and ultimately the very direction of my life.

I am also told, at the same time, that my physical body or material self is what I have in common with the animal kingdom—but if 75% or more of my energy goes toward my material and physical health and wellbeing (as necessary as these are), I am basically starving my potential spiritual self and then wondering why the fruits of my prodigious efforts to attain health, wealth, success, happiness, and the like leave me empty and longing for more. When thinking of this imbalance, I like to recall the phrase shared by Judy Hollis in a workshop: "We can never get enough of what we don't need." If I largely ignore or reject the definition of myself as being primarily a spiritual being, I am going to spend a lot of time, energy, and effort on many things that I do not need.

This line of thinking, of course, is not designed to deny that attending to the true needs of my physical and material life is an absolute necessity. I am, after all, responsible for maintaining all of me, including the physical, mental, emotional, and spiritual aspects. However, how I define myself first and foremost brings balance—or imbalance—to where I place my emphasis and energies. No amount of physical perfection, fame, and fortune can feed my spiritual hunger; in fact, people who amass many worldly possessions often experience a sense of "is that all there is?" However, if this feeling of dissatisfaction is not perceived as neglecting my spiritual needs, I am likely to be driven to amass even more, believing that perhaps two more villas, more fame, or more infamy might give me a sense that I have finally arrived—but "we can never get enough of what we do not need."

Evolutionary Nature of Transformation

> There is only one journey. Going inside yourself.
> —commonly attributed to Rainer Maria Rilke

For the moment, let us return to me and my pre-therapy egogram. The first time I heard the explanation of the PAC circles diagram in a therapy group, I became so upset that I cried on the way home. In response to my husband's solicitous inquiry, I sobbed, "You know those circles they drew up there? I am missing one of those!" It was as if I had suddenly discovered I was missing a limb. Of course, this was an emotional and exaggerated response, but definitely not devoid of truth: my Free Child was rather emaciated and in need of attention. My response was also characteristic of my thought patterns at the time, which were rather black and white, or all or nothing. If there was any fault or blame to be ascribed, I would jump up to claim that it was mine, and then proceed to feel oppressed and depressed. As I write this, I feel tender compassion for the "me" who was so lost and considered her "prison of self" to be reality.

While the Free Child had been neglected, the Critical Parent reigned. Below, I offer some examples of how the dominant Critical Parent functioned in my system. The executive summary, however, is that anything that was labeled "duty" was sanctioned, and was to be obeyed and carried out. Any fun and enjoyment could only be eked out as an accidental by-product; there seemed to be little permission to have fun for fun's sake.

One result of this inner "dictatorship" was that weekends were often my most difficult time; in retrospect, I understand why that was so. During the week, my time was more structured (work, taking my kids to school, etc.); therefore, there was some relief from the nonstop demands of my Critical Parent because I was carrying out my duties. On the weekends, when there was less structure and some fun could be had, my Critical Parent ruled with a vengeance: for instance, I would make long "to-do" lists that could not realistically be carried out—there just were not enough hours in the day. Still, I would try to do everything, and by the end of the weekend I was exhausted and dissatisfied because I had not completed my list; I could not be pleased with what I had accomplished. A sad and frustrating by-product of this manifestation was that I demanded that other family members participate in this frenzy of activity. It could be seen as misery liking company! How could they, who had plenty of access to their Free Child parts, want to watch cartoons and have fun when there was no such inner permission for me to enjoy a pleasurable activity?!

As I mentioned in the previous section, when there are too many directives from Parent, even when they are lofty and praiseworthy, the Child has two options for a response: they can explode (active rebellion) or implode (passive rebellion). Since I was a "good girl," bound and determined to please my parents, whose demands seemed to align with what the Faith was prescribing, active rebellion was out of the question. Therefore, over time and gradually, without the conscious awareness of my Adult, I developed a stance of passivity and depression. Occasionally, this stance manifested during these weekends as a lack of energy, and I would not be able to do anything on those very long "to-do" lists. This fatigue was a coping mechanism to dodge, albeit temporarily, the never-ending demands of my Critical Parent.

As with any coping mechanism, the cost/benefit ratio did not promote health or happiness. The benefit was that it provided me some respite from the constant "doing," because in my system, ill health was an acceptable and legitimate excuse for resting. The cost was that it was not life enhancing; there was a sense that I was cheating because I was not *really* sick, which led to more self-recrimination and guilt. So, when the good Bahá'í therapist summarized her findings at the end of my first therapy session by saying, "Fafar, you need to learn to have more fun," I was totally confused. How could this be a reasonable intervention from a therapist? I was also somewhat at a loss because, having been duty-bound for so long, I told myself I didn't know how to have fun—or know where to begin!

Later on, in my practice, I observed many of these coping mechanisms, which at once demonstrated the ingenious intervention of the survival-oriented human being as well as its limitations. I remember one patient in particular, who I will call X, who came to me because of severe headaches; since her physician had not found any physiological cause for them, she had been referred to me. In-depth exploratory questions did not yield much helpful information, but under hypnosis, which I found very helpful as an adjunct tool in certain cases, X revealed a wealth of information.

I constructed this dialogue with her subconscious mind by respectfully asking to speak to the part of her that gave her those extraordinary headaches. I also praised this part by stating that I was sure that she meant well, and asked her to please share with me how she was "taking care" of X by causing the headaches. This part told me that the patient was a workaholic—a single parent with a very demanding job. She worked long, intensive hours, often taking sandwiches for lunch so she could eat them without taking a break. At the end of the exhausting day, she would bring home more work, which she picked up after taking care of her kids. After a few hours of sleep, she would start the routine all over again.

"So," said this part, "I saw that she was killing herself, so I gave her the excruciating headaches, which gave her no choice but to lie down and stop working! And recently, I had to accelerate my assistance by giving her blurry vision as she was driving to somehow get her attention!" Wow! This client and I were both awed and blown away by the clarity of this revelation, which had been hidden or veiled from her conscious mind. During subsequent sessions, parts of which were still under hypnosis, I once again thanked this part for sharing with me and for its hard work on X's behalf. Then I shared with this part that although its intentions were noble and in fact life-saving, they were also very costly to X, and that now I was here on the scene to help X take much better care of herself so that the headaches, as a means of rest, would become unnecessary. I asked it, respectfully, if it would be willing to slow down its activities and observe X as she developed healthier habits of self-care. X, now having a greater appreciation for and understanding of the inner workings of her own mind, gradually changed many of her behaviors; eventually, the headaches all but disappeared. I found hypnosis, for which I had received intensive training through the Milton Erickson Foundation, an awe-inspiring tool for my therapeutic work. As shown through my story about X, hypnosis confirmed for me, over and over, that the patient holds the problem as well as the core of the solution, and that ultimately the power to heal is potentially within the patient.

So, having gained firsthand knowledge of the inner workings of my own drama with the help of my therapist, I was gradually able to start altering and ameliorating my own PAC circles, with a lot of practice in her therapy groups. After significant exposure to theory and practice, I was able to modify my pre-therapy egogram as well, although I know that this will be an ongoing process—I will always have to keep my Critical Parent in check, keep the Adult on the job, develop more Nurturing Parent, continuously reduce Adaptive Child/Rebellious Child behavior, and assert explicitly my rights and my wishes instead of engaging in "passive

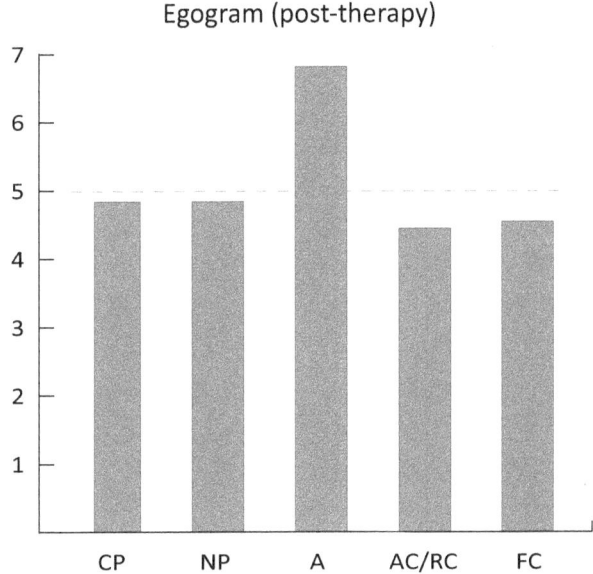

Figure 7. CP = Critical Parent; NP = Nurturing Parent; A = Adult; AC/RC = Adapted Child/Rebellious Child; FC = Free Child. Adapted from *Egograms: How I See You and You See Me*, by Jack Dusay (1977).

rebellion." As a result of these modifications, the Free Child started to blossom, joyfully and spontaneously. My updated egogram is shown in Figure 7.

Like most transformative processes, these changes in my egogram were based on identifying the problem areas, making a commitment to change them, and then practicing, practicing, practicing new behavior.

In Part III, I will be introducing some of the concepts that I have come to call "tools for transformation." These were truly the alphabet—the building blocks without which I would not have been able to "strive to translate that which hath been written into reality and action" (Bahá'u'lláh, *Gleanings*, 250).

Part III
Tools for Transformation

Every trade has its particular and necessary tools; the process of spiritual transformation is no different. In the following section, I will be introducing vital concepts, theories, and practices that guide and facilitate this process. I will also highlight these tools as necessary components and guides for "translating that which hath been written into reality and action" (Bahá'u'lláh, Gleanings, 250). These are tools that I find helpful when navigating the little hills and valleys of everyday life.

The Divine Owner's Manual: Who God Says I Am

> The purpose of the one true God, exalted be His Glory, in revealing Himself unto men is to lay bare those gems that lie hidden within the mine of their true and inmost selves.
> —Bahá'u'lláh (*Gleanings*, 287)

Oh my God! Really? So, if I were to bring this to the personal level, which is really the primary domain for which I am responsible, I could say that my Creator revealed Himself to me so that I would become aware of who I am and what gifts and treasures He has deposited within me?! Several notions are implied here:

1. The "gems" are in everyone, not just in a few people. If I deny or remain ignorant of the gems within me, my self-assessment is at odds with the "Owner's Manual." Also, if I delude myself by not being aware of the "gems" in others, I have again missed the point; therefore, my answer to the second Basic Question of "Who are the others?" will be off-kilter and erroneous.

2. The word "mine" implies that these gems are hidden. So, in the physical realm, if we know or believe that there are "gems"

hidden somewhere in the earth, we set up a way to excavate them. This process is often long, messy, and arduous, requiring lots of patience and persistence.

3. The "Owner's Manual" also tells me that my Creator wants to "lay bare" these gems that He has deposited in me, which lets me know that if I want to align my will with His, I should start digging, now, because He wants me to see His handiwork.

4. These newly discovered gems within are in rough form, just as they are in the physical realm. They must be extracted, cleansed, and polished before they can reveal their true luster. Remember these words: "All that which ye potentially possess can, however, be manifested only as a result of your own volition" (Bahá'u'lláh, *Gleanings*, 149).

5. God is speaking of our "true and inmost selves," which implies that I can construct a false outer self in my ignorance and unawareness of the "Owner's Manual."

There are two ways in which I could act as my own worst enemy in this process of discovering and developing the latent potentialities within me. The most common pitfall is (1) not believing that there is anything of value within me and therefore not "mine" at all, in which case my gems remain hidden and undiscovered, depriving me and others of their shine. Or, I might go mining, but (2) act as if I determine what should be buried within me; for example, let's say that I think I will find gold, but at the end of all my digging I find only rubies or coal. I may go away disappointed and quit digging altogether, or stubbornly continue to dig in the hope that I strike gold. This attitude is the height of arrogance and ignorance, because what I am really saying is that I don't approve of the Perfect Creator's work, because I, the imperfect puny creature, would have done it differently.

To avoid these pitfalls, it might be helpful for me to bring it down to the personal level by (1) fortifying my absolute belief and faith that God does not lie—therefore, there are treasures deposited in me, and then (2) make it my single-minded task to dig, dig, dig. When I (3) discover whatever treasures are there, those talents, proclivities, and capabilities, I should give praise and gratitude for my portion, and (4) begin polishing my gems or perfecting those once-hidden qualities and attributes with a grateful heart. One day, I will (5) joyfully offer my particular gems in service to humanity—"this is what *I* bring to the table"—presented not with arrogance, but with joy, humility, and gladness.

In this mining process, comparisons with others can be deadly showstoppers. In my workshops, I offered this example: if the seeds sown within me are for a daisy, but I enviously look at someone else who is a rose and try to shape myself into a rose, I will never become a rose—and I will be a pathetic-looking daisy! The observation of others' gifts and talents, on the other hand, could well inspire me to discover and develop my own in addition to appreciating and celebrating theirs, which is tantamount to celebrating our Creator.

It is my privilege and responsibility to become an expert on myself. From a letter dated May 12, 1925, written on behalf of Shoghi Effendi to an individual believer, it is stated that

> Each of us is responsible for one life only and that is our own. Each of us is immeasurably far from being "perfect as our Heavenly Father is perfect" and the task of perfecting our own life and character is one that requires all our attention, our willpower and energy. If we allow our attention and energy to be taken up in efforts to keep others right and remedy their faults, we are wasting precious time....On no subject are the Bahá'í teachings more emphatic than on the necessity to abstain from fault-finding, while being ever eager to discover and root out our own faults and overcome our own failings. (Shoghi Effendi, "Living the Life," 3–4)

Another way of looking at this process is to think of oneself as a gardener tending a young plant. Becoming an expert on myself means not only discovering potentially what kind of plant I am, but also patiently exploring what kind of soil, lighting, fertilizer, and care I need to thrive. Once again, though—comparisons can be deadly! Let's say I am a plant that produces magnificent flowers just once a year, but I share a garden with plants that seem to bloom nonstop. If I experience myself as inferior, by way of comparison, I might despair and become so discontent that I neglect myself to the point of shriveling and dying. So, knowing the self cannot be accomplished without a focused, loving, attentive attitude. On the other hand, if I myself am the nonstop bloomer and compare myself to the other plant, I may develop a false sense of superiority and miss out on the magnificence of the once-a-year bloomer.

Sometimes, we erroneously equate ignorance of self as selflessness; this equivalence is born from a belief that not only are there no gems within, there are horrible things within that are best hidden. Alternately, I might simply not want to take on the arduous task of mining, which the "Owner's Manual" says is linked to my primary life purpose. Because I cannot acknowledge that I am engaging in work-avoidance, I sublimate my less noble intentions into an attitude of grandeur and false humility, which says I am so transcendent that I do not need to know or focus on myself, or that my humility does not allow me to spend time getting to know myself. This stance is contrary to the passage cited earlier: "True loss is for him whose days have been spent in utter ignorance of his self" (Bahá'u'lláh, *Tablets of Bahá'u'lláh*, 156).

In fact, the Guardian states that faith alone is not sufficient in becoming a true Bahá'í; it needs to go hand-in-hand with character development:

> *There is a difference between character and faith; it is often hard to accept this fact and put up with it, but the fact remains that a person may believe in and love the Cause — even to being ready to die for it — and yet not have a good personal character, or possess traits at variance with the Teachings. We should try to change, to let the Power of God help recreate us, make us true Bahá'ís indeed as well as in belief. But the process is slow, sometimes it never happens because the individual does not try hard enough. But these things cause us suffering and are a test to us and our fellow-believers.* (Shoghi Effendi, in Hornby, *Lights of Guidance*, 76)

For me, this passage from Shoghi Effendi was illuminating in its support and validation of the process of spiritual transformation. In it, he seems to emphasize several points: (1) faith alone is not enough, (2) we need God's help for the process of aligning our behavior with our faith and belief, (3) individual initiative in undertaking this difficult task is crucial to this alignment, and (4) when we neglect this vital process of change, we ourselves and others suffer the results.

There are many barriers, internal and external, that challenge this process of aligning ourselves with the mandates of the Divine Owners' Manual. We will next focus on another vital tool, the "Okay Corral," which highlights a variety of internal barriers developed in early childhood that are based on a particular child's external experiences.

The "Okay Corral" — Another Vital Practical Tool for Transformation

> It is never too late to be what you might have been.
> —commonly attributed to George Eliot

The "Okay Corral," a significant element of Transactional Analysis theory, was developed by Franklin Ernst (in Stewart and Joines, *TA Today*, 118-23). The theory underlying this idea is that we come to the world feeling okay about ourselves and others, highly motivated to survive and thrive, and trusting that the environment will give us what we need. During the first crucial five years of our lives, we gradually move away from this initial and unexamined sense of okay-ness (I'm okay/you're okay) and assume one of three dysfunctional quadrants as our "basic life position." We select a particular quadrant based on a set of givens over which we have no control, as well as our own individual interpretation of this set of assumptions. This is another way of looking at the child's efforts to find answers to the Three Basic Questions (Who am I? Who are the others? How will I make it?). The four quadrants of the "Okay Corral" are as follows:

- Quadrant 1: I'm not okay/You're okay;
- Quadrant 2: I'm not okay/You're not okay;
- Quadrant 3: I'm okay/You're not okay;
- Quadrant 4: I'm okay/You're okay.

Figure 8 (next page) shows the four quadrants and describes their basic slogan, predominant feeling, and extreme behavioral manifestations of each position.

As I have taught and thought about the "Okay Corral," I have changed the shape and added the notion of "blame." In my version of the diagram, it is easier for me to see Quadrants 1 and 3 as opposites—but really, they

"Okay Corral"

I- U+
"Getting away from"

Predominant feeling:	Sadness, depression
Extreme behavioral manifestation:	Suicidal

I+ U+
"Getting on with"

Predominant feeling:	No predominant feelings; there is open expression of any and all feelings appropriate to the situation at hand.
Extreme beharioral manifestation:	*No prescribed behavior*, other than autonomy, wholeness, fulfillment.

I- U-
"Getting nowhere"

Predominant feeling:	Depression, despair
Extreme behavioral manifestation:	Insanity

I+ U-
"Getting rid of"

Predominant feeling:	Anger (experienced as justifiable)
Extreme behavioral manifestation:	Homicidal

Figure 8. I+ = I'm okay; I- = I'm not okay; U+ = you're okay; U- = you're not okay. Adapted from "Okay Corral: The Grid for Get-On-With," by Franklin Ernst (1971, 33–42).

are mirror images; Quadrants 2 and 4 are opposites. See the diagram of my version of the "Okay Corral" in Figure 9.

As mentioned, each quadrant has its own set of thinking, feeling, and behaving; here, I offer brief descriptions of these quadrants. The first quadrant (I- U+) is labeled "I'm not okay, you're okay" or GAF (Getting Away From). In this quadrant, I see myself as "not okay, as less than, and inferior," but I see others as "okay and superior to myself." The predominant feeling in this quadrant is sadness and depression; since I consider myself less-than, my feelings of sadness are borne from this belief and the accompanying behaviors consist of self-sabotage, not standing up for myself, allowing others to step all over me, and so on. When I am in

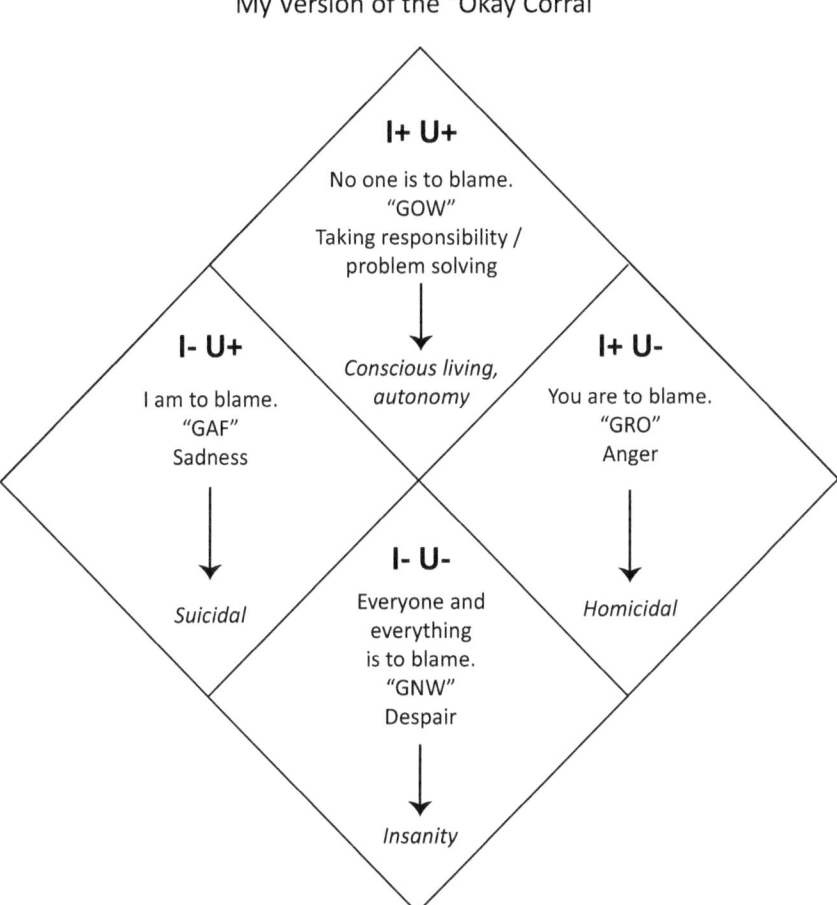

Figure 9. My modified "Okay Corral." I+ = I'm okay; I- = I'm not okay; U+ = you're okay; U- = you're not okay. GOW = Getting On With; GAF = Getting Away From; GNW = Getting Nowhere; GRO = Getting Rid Of. Figure adaptation based on Ernst, "The Okay Corral," 33–42. Figure by author.

the company of others, I compare myself to them—often unfairly—and fall short in my own eyes, so I prefer to isolate myself (i.e., "getting away from"). The extreme behavioral manifestation of this quadrant is "suicidal," which has its own twisted black-and-white logic: "If I am not okay and others are, then eliminating myself altogether is a kind of solution, all will be well if I'm gone!" Having said that, there is a long continuum on which my feelings, thoughts, and behaviors may fall; similarly, there are many degrees of "suicidal" behavior: any time I don't attend to my physical, mental, and spiritual needs, I am in essence saying that "I am not as worthy of life, of my own attention and affection, as others are." So, I am often self-deprecating, spending inordinate amounts of time and energy taking care of others while neglecting my own wants and needs. The term "pathological humility" could be an apt description of this stance.

Furthermore, I will begin to experience this sense of not okay-ness as an intrinsic definition of myself, and nearly all the decisions I make will be tainted by my "Basic Life Position" in one way or another. As I make more self-sabotaging decisions and suffer the consequences, my initial belief of not okay-ness is confirmed. As a result, I often find myself victimized by others, without awareness or acknowledgement of how I participate in my own victimization.

The second quadrant can be summed up as (I- U-) — "I'm not okay, you're not okay" or GNW (Getting Nowhere). In this quadrant, I see neither myself nor the other as okay, so the predominant feeling is despair: if I am not okay and neither is anybody else, it is all senseless. The extreme behavioral manifestation is "insanity" — life is so confusing and confounding that my "solution" becomes, to some extent, taking leave of my own senses. If life seems so incomprehensible and crazy-making, why not let go of sanity? This outcome, too, appears on a continuum. Any time my rational thinking stops and I am beset by a fog of confusion, believing that I can't think clearly, I am in this quadrant. I might use drugs or alcohol to help me escape from this nonsensical reality, and when I am in this quadrant, I tend to use/abuse self and others with no-win outcomes.

Often, the behavior of groups of people who have been systemically and systematically oppressed over a long period of time can fall into this quadrant. One might speculate that an example could be Black on Black crime. It seems to confirm the internalized notion that since I am not okay and you are not okay, I will eliminate you and have myself killed in the process or spend the rest of my life in prison, a lose-lose proposition. Another less extreme manifestation could be women putting other women down, hurting both in the process. As a woman, I might also fall prey to the stereotypical cultural injunction that promotes the notion that women are "illogical" by nature because they are too "emotional." If I, as a woman, don't fully utilize my God-given power of intellect with my capacity to feel deeply, I am confirming the myth that men are more logical than women.

In the third quadrant (I+ U-) — "I'm okay, you're not okay" or GRO (Getting Rid Of) — I see myself as okay and the other as not okay. The predominant feeling is anger, which I experience as "justifiable" anger. In this quadrant, I will have lists and categories of people I see as not okay: "If it weren't for [insert group of people here], life would be good." Following this black-and-white logic to its behavioral extreme leads us to homicide — "If I get rid of you, my life will be fine." There is a sense of entitlement and inherent superiority associated with this quadrant, based on a multitude of variables, such as race, gender, ethnicity, education, class, and so on. Unfortunately, there are many historic examples of this stance, which when combined with unlimited power and authority has produced catastrophic tragedies; see, for one example, Hitler's decision that entire categories of humanity needed to be eliminated.

The fourth Quadrant (I+ U+) — "I'm okay, you're okay" or GOW (Getting On With) — is the only sane and life-enhancing position. There is no predominant feeling associated with this quadrant other than a deeply rooted sense of peace and contentment. In this quadrant, I have full access to the basic four families of feelings — glad, mad, sad, and scared — which allows me to respond to life events with appropriate feelings. In other words, I am free from a dysfunctional Basic Life Position. Predictably, there is no catastrophic extreme behavioral manifestation; this position is made apparent through a conscious, responsible, and authentic life. If I occupy this quadrant, I respect and honor myself just as I afford the same respect and honor to others. I neither compare myself unfairly to others, which would result in depression and despair, nor do I need to perceive myself as superior to others and exhibit an inflated sense of self. Unlike a denizen of the third quadrant, my sense of okay-ness is not contingent on others not being okay.

Now that the "Okay Corral" has been described, I have a few more thoughts about this particular "tool for transformation." None of us is permanently stuck in a particular dysfunctional quadrant; over the course of a single day, we may visit each quadrant as we react to news or events. For instance, I may hear about a major accomplishment of a friend or acquaintance, and my inner Critical Parent may say something like, "Look at what so-and-so has done; what's the matter with you?" This response may take me to the I- U+ quadrant.

Then, let's suppose that I am unjustly criticized by a boss at work or a family member at home, which will move me to the I- U- position. In this quadrant, I may feel hopeless — "No matter what I do, nothing works, so why keep trying?" Later in the day, I may hear something in the news about some protesters, assume a superior I+ U- position, and be "justifiably" angry: "I wish these people would just shut up and let us live in peace; what else do they want?" If I then experience a genuine act of kindness, or have a moment of prayer or meditation, or find myself moved by the beauty of nature or music, I may attain the I+ U+ quadrant, where I actually feel inner peace and calm. There is no agitation of comparisons, rating, or ranking. I feel okay about myself and I experience the fundamental okay-ness of everyone else, a win-win outcome.

Although everyone experiences the various quadrants to some degree or another from time to time, the "Okay Corral" theory states that for each individual there is one dysfunctional quadrant that serves as their home base—and given enough stress, they are likely to go to that particular quadrant. We all may go 'round and 'round the "Okay Corral," but each of us spend at least over 50% of our time in our "favorite" dysfunctional quadrant (Stewart and Joines, *TA Today*, 122).

At first glance, one may feel that the I+ U- quadrant might be better than the other two dysfunctional options, because at least the occupant of this quadrant feels okay about themselves. However, a closer examination reveals that this self-acceptance or okay-ness is very conditional, because their okay-ness is contingent on someone (or someones) not being okay. A person in this I+ U- quadrant is not okay being equal to others, and needs to establish and maintain a sense of superiority in order to feel okay. This means that even though the person's attitude and behavior may be one of entitlement and superiority, underneath it all they feel not okay about themselves. See, for instance, the playground "bully" who tries to make up for his own sense of inferiority or cowardice by physically or verbally beating up on someone weaker than himself.

Therefore, the only safe, sane, real place is the fourth quadrant, where one knows and accepts themselves with their strengths and weaknesses. There, one can accept others as fellow travelers on life's journey with their own set of strengths and weaknesses. This realization, in and of itself, brings one to a state of true humility, not "pathological humility." So, if I want to be responsible for my own physical, mental, emotional, and spiritual wellbeing, it behooves me to increase the time I spend in the I+ U+ quadrant.

'Abdu'l-Bahá states that there is no prison greater than the prison of self: "When one is released from the prison of self, that is indeed release, for that is the greater prison" (*'Abdu'l-Bahá in London*, 120). I refer to the three dysfunctional quadrants as the various cells of the "prison of self." Before I had the "Okay Corral" concept to work with, when I read about the "prison of self" in the Writings, I only (and automatically) thought about it in terms of a person being full of himself—in other words, the I+ U- position. While this is true enough, I now see these three dysfunctional quadrants as prisons of self. Anytime that my self-concept or my concept of others are at odds with who God says I am and who they are, I am suffering from "vain imaginings." My prison cell (i.e., dysfunctional quadrant) may be different from yours, but we are both still in a *prison of self*.

Therefore, once again we should recognize the loving wisdom and the absolute necessity behind the mandate of knowing ourselves. In the three cells of the prison of self, we are living in a reactive mode dominated by a set of patterns of thinking, feeling, and behaving that we, as children, adopted in reaction to a set of givens over which we had no control. Remember, we came into the world with a survival mandate, so we adopted—with all the wisdom and maturity of four- and five-year-olds—whatever we felt was necessary for our survival in our particular familial setting. That is why changing our patterns of thinking, feeling, and behaving is so difficult; as maladaptive as these patterns may be, a part of us feels that they are absolutely necessary for our survival. We cling to them tenaciously because they are the only inner maps we have as our answer to the third Basic Question: "How will I make it?" This ingrained, hard-to-revise map is why compassion and patience toward ourselves, as well as others, are absolutely necessary components of change and transformation.

There is a passage that seems to speak directly about this process of solidifying our initial reactive patterns of thinking and feeling until they become synonymous with "reality":

> Imagination is one of our greatest powers and a most difficult one to rule. Imagination is the father of superstition…we are led astray by imagination, even in violation of will and reason. It is our test power. We are tested by our ability to control and subdue it.…Imagination is our greatest misleader. We hold to it until it becomes fixed in memory. Then we hold to it the stronger, believing it to be fact. It is a great power of the soul, but without value unless rightly controlled and guided.[3]

To me, it is very exciting and affirming to think that some of the "truths" about self, others, and the nature of life that I carry in my head are erroneous and outdated; they are nothing but an inner map adopted by me as a child. If these notions remain unexamined by an objective and fair-minded adult version of me, then I continue to remain a victim of a road map that at best may be obsolete and, at worst, out-and-out harmful to my being. Even if the initial givens of my family of origin were benign and/or praise-worthy, my blind obedience lacks an element of choice; therefore, I

---

[3] This quote is taken from pilgrims' notes from one of 'Abdu'l-Bahá's talks (see Julia Grundy, *Ten Days in the Light of 'Akká*, 29). "Pilgrims' notes" are recollections by an individual of words they heard from 'Abdu'l-Bahá, but which should not be taken as His exact words or considered authoritative.

would be living an unexamined life, which often lacks the joy and vitality born of personal discovery and conviction.

As Bahá'ís, we believe that humanity as a whole is entering the age of maturity. The role and responsibility of spiritual enlightenment and guidance formerly assigned to priests or other religious leaders are now bestowed on each individual. This assignment is at once challenging and exciting. It is challenging because we have to part ways with habitual and therefore comfortable ways of being and doing; it is exciting because we are creating something new.

For me personally, nothing is more exhilarating and empowering than attempting to bring my "being" and "doing" in harmony with the latest edition of the "Owner's Manual." As I walk on this path, I feel that I am fulfilling my "raison d'être" *to know and to worship God* by gaining knowledge of my true self; my humble and often painful, slow, and awkward efforts toward wholeness and authenticity are my own private sacred experiment of aligning myself, both my God-given set of potentialities as well as my limitations, with the guidance of the Divine Owner's Manual. I feel that each of us is invited and urged to present a personal prototype of what He says a new human race should be. So, if we look at the three "dysfunctional" quadrants of the "Okay Corral," we can find numerous passages from the Writings that discredit the erroneous assumptions of the various cells within the "prison of self." I shall cite a few of these.

For the (I- U+) Quadrant—I'm Not Okay, You're Okay:

Dost thou reckon thyself only a puny form when within thee the Universe is folded?

(Bahá'u'lláh, *The Seven Valleys*, 34)

Turn thy sight unto thyself that thou mayest find Me standing within thee, Mighty, Powerful and Self-Subsisting.

(Bahá'u'lláh, *Hidden Words*, 6–7)

Do not look at your own weakness, nay, rely upon the confirmation of the Holy Spirit. Verily it maketh the weak strong, the lowly mighty, the child grown...and the small great.

('Abdu'l-Bahá, *Tablets of 'Abdu'l-Bahá Abbás*, 274)

For the (I- U-) Quadrant—I'm Not Okay, You're Not Okay:

Noble I made thee, wherewith dost thou abase thyself?

(Bahá'u'lláh, *Hidden Words*, 6–7)

One must never consider one's own feebleness...the thought of our own weakness could only bring despair.

('Abdu'l-Bahá, *Paris Talks*, 39)

The afflictions which come to humanity sometimes tend to centre the consciousness upon the limitations, and this is a veritable prison. Release comes by making of the will a Door through which the confirmations of the Spirit come.

('Abdu'l-Bahá, *'Abdu'l-Bahá in London*, 120)

For the (I+ U-) Quadrant—I'm Okay, You're Not Okay:

Beware lest ye prefer your own selves before the Mercy of God...

(Bahá'u'lláh, in *Bahá'í World Faith*, 204)

How couldst thou forget thine own faults and busy thyself with the faults of others? Whoso doeth this is accursed of Me.

(Bahá'u'lláh, *Hidden Words*, 10)

O CHILDREN OF MEN! Know ye not why We created you all from the same dust? That no one should exalt himself over the other.

(Bahá'u'lláh, *Hidden Words*, 20)

O SON OF DUST! Verily I say unto thee; of all men the most negligent is he that disputeth idly and seeketh to advance himself over his brother. Say: O brethren! Let deeds, not words, be your adorning.

(Bahá'u'lláh, *Hidden Words*, 23–24)

O CHILDREN OF DESIRE! Put away the garment of vain glory, and divest yourselves of the attire of haughtiness.

(Bahá'u'lláh, *Hidden Words*, 39)

We are also given numerous clues about the characteristics of this freed self, which is harmonious with the fourth quadrant.

The (I+ U+) Quadrant—I'm Okay, You're Okay:

The whole duty of man in this day is to attain that share of the flood of grace which God poureth forth for him.

(Bahá'u'lláh, *Gleanings*, 8)

For every one of you his paramount duty is to choose for himself that on which no other may infringe and none usurp from him. Such a thing – and to this the Almighty is my witness – is the love of God, could ye but perceive it. Build ye for yourselves such houses as rain and floods can never destroy, which shall protect you from the changes and chances of this life.

(Bahá'u'lláh, *Gleanings*, 261)

You are always in the presence of God. Open the windows of your soul so His presence may be within you.

('Abdu'l-Bahá, quoted in Grundy, *Ten Days in the Light of 'Akká*, 40)

O MY SERVANTS! Ye are the trees of My garden, ye must give forth goodly and wondrous fruits, that ye yourselves and others may profit therefrom.

(Bahá'u'lláh, *Hidden Words*, 51)

O MY FRIEND! Thou art the daystar of the heavens of My holiness, let not the defilement of the world eclipse thy splendor. Rend asunder the veil of heedlessness, that from behind the clouds thou mayest emerge resplendent and array all things with the apparel of life.

(Bahá'u'lláh, *Hidden Words*, 47)

Having discussed the many different ways we can lose track of our essential goodness all at variance with the Divine Owner's Manual's definition of us, we now turn to another mighty tool for transformation called "Feelings as Messengers."

FAM: Feelings as Messengers

> It is terribly amusing how many different climates of feelings
> one can go through in a day.
> —commonly attributed to Anne Morrow Lindbergh

It is time to add another tool to our "tools for transformation" kit. Given that nothing in our creation is random or haphazard, we have to recognize and appreciate that the Perfect Creator has charged us all with the need to meet the exigencies of our brief but highly significant material life, as well as develop potentialities which, if used correctly, would enhance our spiritual growth and development—the main purpose of our physical existence in the first place. Our physical lifespan of up to 100+ years has been compared by 'Abdu'l-Bahá as a gestation period, much like a fetus in the womb. The fetus does not comprehend that the purpose of its existence in the womb is to develop the capacities (e.g., the five senses) that it will need when it is welcomed into this glorious, physical life. The fetus might experience the nine months of gestation as an eternity, an end in itself.

The main distinction between the life of the fetus and our physical life is the power of comprehension and consciousness. Our Creator has bestowed knowledge and guidance on humanity to enhance these capabilities, progressively, through the various Chapters of the Holy Books of Divine Revelation. Unlike the fetus, we are aware that there is an inevitable end to our physical existence. I like the title and, of course, the wonderful content of Dr. John Hatcher's book, *Understanding Death: The Most Important Event of Your Life*. If we choose to remain ignorant of the stated goals for this century-long journey, we become confused and despondent relative to our ultimate death. If we don't comprehend the true meaning of death as it has been progressively revealed through the Scriptures of the world's religions—as a birth into a glorious realm, the nature of which we are not meant nor able to understand, we view death with fear, sadness, confusion, and anger. Needless to say, this attitude toward death has profound ramifications for how we go through this life.

Here, I introduce the tool of FAM: Feelings as Messengers. The concept of Feelings as Messengers was originated by Fanita English ("The Substitution Factor," 1971) and further developed by Felipe Garcia ("Responsivity," 1991).

One of the ways in which our Creator has equipped us to meet the exigencies of this life and responsibly take charge of our own wellbeing is our capacity for experiencing and expressing a number of feelings. In recent years, more attention has been given to the interconnectedness of various systems in our bodies (i.e., the impact of our thoughts and feelings on our physical and mental health), and specific attention has been paid to the necessity of acknowledging and understanding the nature and impact of our feelings. Some have referred to this knowledge as "emotional literacy" or "emotional intelligence."

There have been several attempts to elaborate on the nuances of emotional intelligence. One of these, the Feeling Wheel (Figure 10), is attributed to Dr. Gloria Willcox; it appears in her work, *Feelings: Converting Negatives to Positives*.

This system refers to four basic Families of Feelings: glad, mad, sad, and scared. Sometimes "glad" is broken into three subcategories: joyful, peaceful, and powerful. The notion of the four basic Families of Feelings is analogous to the three primary colors of red, blue, and yellow; while it is possible to make an endless variety of shades, each one is created by mixing these primary colors together. Similarly, there are myriad emotions on the Feeling Wheel, but all of them stem from the four Families of Feelings.

Another element of Feelings as Messengers is the notion that each of these Families of Feelings sends us a specific message regarding what we are experiencing, as well as a corrective and prescriptive action that will bring us back to a state of equilibrium. The suggested messages of each Family of Feeling, along with its prescriptive action, are outlined below.

- **Glad:** Here, the message is "Everything is a-okay." The corrective action can be summarized with one of these ideas: *Keep on keeping on, whatever I'm doing is working*, or *no further action is required at this time*.

- **Mad:** "There is a violation of me and my boundaries." This transgression might be physical, emotional, or psychological. Corrective action here relates to the need to set or re-set my boundaries.

Spiritual Transformation | 71

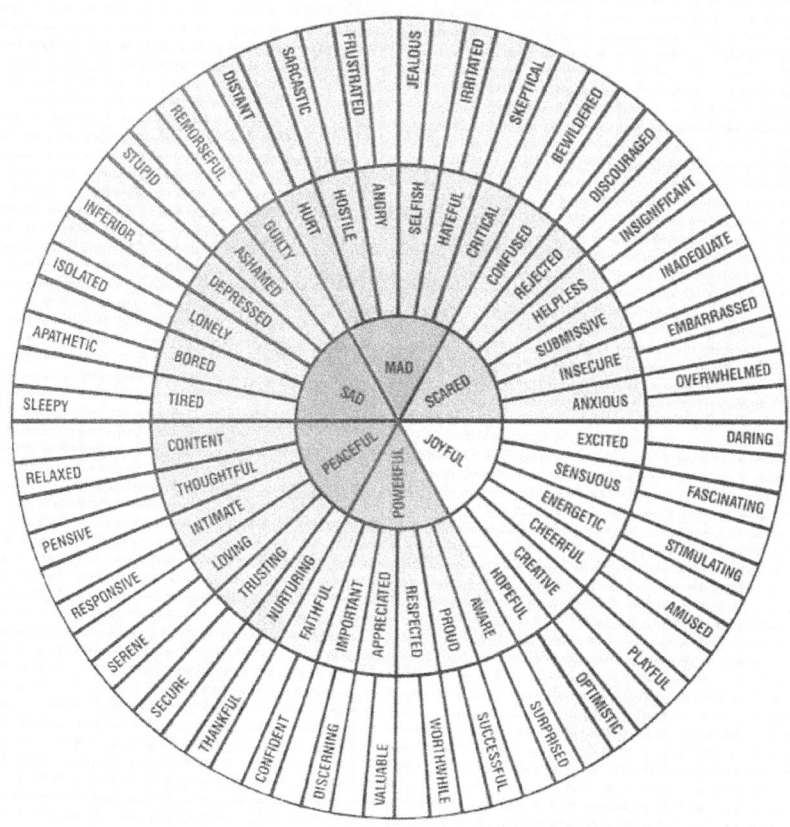

The Feeling Wheel

Figure 10. The Feeling Wheel, developed by Dr. Gloria Willcox, appeared in "The Feeling Wheel: A Tool for Expanding Awareness of Emotions and Increasing Spontaneity and Intimacy" (1982, 276). Diagram reprinted with generous permission from the author.

- **Sad:** "There is a loss or an anticipation of a loss." Taking corrective action means acknowledging a need for time and space to mourn the loss and take in nurturance from myself or others.
- **Scared:** "There is danger." Corrective action requires finding protection.

The following are some typical examples of messages, and appropriate and inappropriate corrective action attempts:

- **Mad:** A woman is in a predominantly male work setting where one or more of the men often tell off-color, sexist jokes in her presence. An inappropriate action would be for her to address the would-be comics with "You are such a sexist pig, I can't stand you!" An appropriate response, however, might go like this: "David, when you tell these types of jokes, I feel offended and angry. I am requesting that you not tell these jokes in my presence in the future." What makes the first response inappropriate is that it, too, is offensive by virtue of name-calling; often, this kind of action will escalate to further defensive/offensive exchanges, leading to both parties going away feeling mutually attacked and angrier than before. The appropriate action doesn't escalate: the offended party describes the offensive action and its impact on her, and sets her boundary without a counterattack. As a result, she feels empowered, intact, and whole because she has stood up for herself. The impact on the "offending" party is often disarming, since he has not been blamed or attacked but has been presented with a request that implicitly invites him to be more aware of the impact of his actions on others. This approach preserves the dignity of both parties. Of course, this approach does not always guarantee a neutral or positive response from the offending party, but regardless of his response, the offended person can be at peace because she has done her best to protect her boundaries by asserting her rights without attempting to wound the other party.
- **Sad:** Person A has just received news about the death of a friend. An inappropriate action here would entail discounting her feelings and delaying any form of mourning. This action could be accompanied by erroneous thoughts, such as "If I start crying, I'll never be able to stop!" This person would also keep the sadness to herself, based on another erroneous thought along the lines of "Nobody cares how I feel" or "It won't help to talk about it; what is it going to change?" Studies have repeatedly

shown that repressing our feelings can have moderate to severe negative impacts on our health—it is said that "unshed tears show up somewhere else in the body." An appropriate action would be for her to acknowledge the impact of this loss and the depth of her sadness; she needs to give herself time and space to mourn. Crying is quite an appropriate response, regardless of some cultural norms that discourage such an open expression of feelings. If possible, she could share the news with another person, and receive the comfort of empathy and nurturance in any form that feels good to her.

- **Scared:** My friend has just confided to me that their parent has received an Alzheimer's diagnosis. If I respond inappropriately, while talking to that friend, I might start worrying about my parents or even become anxious myself when I can't instantly recall a name or a date. Instead of sharing my fear with anyone, I might then imagine any number of catastrophic scenarios. A more appropriate action would be to get the necessary information to allay my fears by talking to my health professional, and, if appropriate, take preventive measures to safeguard my own mental health. I might also remind myself that whatever lies ahead, no matter how severe or scary, I can always rely on the knowledge that a caring and omniscient God will give me the ability to bear that burden.

Although the correct action makes sense in these examples, there are two major potential obstacles that greatly impact how we use our feelings to enhance our quality of life. These are the two "givens" over which we have no control: the culture and the particular family into which we are born. Each culture has its own dictates, based on its beliefs and values, on how feelings should or should not be experienced and expressed. Although I am intimately familiar with several cultures, here I will focus mostly on the cultural heritage of the United States.

One of the most significant contributors to how feelings are regarded and expressed is the cultural attitudes toward each gender. Having presented a variety of workshops on topics such as racism, sexism, and spiritual transformation to a wide range of participants (e.g., churches, corporations, educational institutions, Bahá'í schools) for over 30 years, I have come to some conclusions. One of the exercises that would always yield quick results in revealing our cultural heritage was putting two columns on a flip chart with the headings of *Feelings* and *Thinking*. Then, participants would be asked to state whatever came to their mind relative to these two headings. The instructions stated that this list was not about how things *should* be—as in what was right, what was wrong, or even what their own personal beliefs and opinions were—but rather a list based on their experience of this culture. A list similar to the following would develop (Figure 11), often in just a few minutes.

Feelings	Thinking
Messy	Good
Histrionic	Calm and collected
Confusing	Clear
Illogical	Logical
Out of control	Under control
Irrational	Rational
Hindrance to problem solving	Asset in problem solving
Weak	Strong
Childish	Mature

Figure 11. List developed by workshop participants reflecting cultural attitudes toward "feelings" and "thinking."

Then we (often my husband and I, or other workshop co-facilitators) would ask them to consider the list they had just developed in terms of the two genders; invariably, the participants placed women in the "feelings" column and men in the "thinking" one. Subsequently, we would point out that this should not be surprising, because this action's roots go back to the belief that women are less valuable than men. Consciously or not, they have been historically—despite much progress—relegated to second-class citizenship even in modern U.S. culture, though as a society we have made great strides toward gender equality. Yet and still, U.S. culture devalues those qualities, innate or culturally attributed, which are more characteristic of women. Although the reality is that the inherent capacities to feel and to think have been equally endowed by our Creator to both genders, our historical beliefs and attitudes about the inferiority of women have affected women's intellectual development through lack of opportunities—in this culture and other cultures around the world.

It might be helpful at this juncture to introduce another concept or tool known as "Levels of Oppression," which was developed by VISIONS. This concept states that any form of prejudice or "ism"—rac*ism*, sex*ism*, class*ism*, and so on—manifests itself at four levels: Personal, Interpersonal,

Four Levels of Oppression

Personal		Cultural
Beliefs Feelings Attitudes • Caught or taught • In or out of awareness *"What do I think and feel about others who are different?"*		Values Standards World view Unwritten rules *"How do my cultural values discount and discredit others?"*
	Racism Sexism Classism Ageism etc.	
Institutional		**Interpersonal**
Laws Policies • Procedures that systematically result in inequities within an agency, organization, or society *"How does the institution favor the majority group?"*		Behaviors Interactions • Based on personal-level beliefs, feelings, attitudes • Can be intentional or unintentional *"How do I behave toward others who are different?"*

Figure 12. The Four Levels of Oppression. Data adapted from VISIONS training materials. Reprinted with permission from VISIONS Inc.

Institutional, and Cultural (Figure 12). The beliefs, feelings, and attributes of these "ism" manifestations can be conscious or unconscious.

Putting these four Levels of Oppression to work in terms of sexism, for example, might look something like the content in Figure 13 (next page).

This cursory overview of how a belief in the inherent inferiority of women might show up at the four levels allows us to more closely examine their effects relative to the expression of feelings. Armed with this knowledge, we return to the workshop exercise.

After sharing information about the four basic Families of Feelings, we would ask the participants to share their perception of how culture impacts

Four Levels of Oppression: Sexism Example

Personal	Cultural
Beliefs Feelings Attitudes	Values Standards World view Unwritten rules
• Belief that women are inherently inferior to men • Notion that women are too emotional and incapable of logical thinking	• Women portrayed as sex objects, over-emphasis of physical attributes • Women not taken seriously in business or politics until recently • Devaluation of qualities and characteristics in which women may be stronger (i.e., intuition)

Sexism

Institutional	Interpersonal
Laws Policies	Behaviors Interactions
• Wage disparity: In 2018, women earn $0.85 while men earn $1 for the same work • Organizational glass ceilings • Lack of access to information and networking (e.g., informal golf outings, happy hours)	• Treatment of women could range from abusive to paternalistic and condescending • Lack of recognition or respect for women's contributions in the workplace and society at large

Figure 13. The Four Levels of Oppression, as seen through the lens of sexism. Information adapted from VISIONS training materials. Reprinted with permission from VISIONS Inc.

each gender relative to expressions of feelings. Again, this question did not entail an evaluation of rightness or wrongness; it was meant to inspire reflection about participants' cultural norms. When asked, "Which Family of Feelings are men allowed, or even encouraged to express freely?", the answer was always primarily "Mad" and, secondarily, Glad—as long as there was not too much of it, because then they would not be taken seriously and could be seen as "silly or sissy." Of course, the root of "sissy" is *sister*—connoting *female, weaker,* and *unworthy of a man's demeanor.* When asked which Family of Feelings were taboo for men, without hesitation participants replied by saying Sad and Scared. Culturally, these two feeling families were perceived as and linked to weakness, which is at odds with the cultural image of men as being strong to the point of being invincible; men are stoic, rugged individuals who can do without aid and assistance from others.

When asked the same question about women, there was ready agreement that the culture sanctions Glad, Sad, and Scared; for them, the taboo feelings family was Mad. It can be readily perceived that these cultural norms are deeply rooted in cherished ancestral beliefs and values. Like many cultural standards, they have become so ingrained that they are experienced as natural or "reality."

Historically, and up to a point even now, these gendered Family of Feelings assignments have gone hand-in-glove with sexism. It is becoming to the "weaker" gender to feel and express the feeling families of Sad and Scared, which then conveniently supports the perception of men as the "stronger" gender who can support, protect, and rescue their "weaker" counterparts. Women are given ample permission to express the feelings of Glad, because there is cultural support, and indeed expectation, for women to be pleasant and to bring joy and peace to others—no matter whether the feelings are genuine. When women express Glad without inwardly feeling peaceful, powerful, and joyful in order to fulfill their assigned cultural role, we refer to it as "glossed-over Glad."

This gendered categorization of the Family of Feelings, based in the illusion of the inherent superiority of males over females, has had far-reaching negative results for both genders in terms of physical, mental, and emotional health and wellbeing. The Bahá'í Writings state that the bird of humanity, which has two wings that symbolize feminine and masculine elements, cannot soar until both wings are equally developed and fully functioning.

Our perfect Creator has given us the capacity to have feelings so that we can fully enjoy life and take charge of our own physical, mental, emotional, and spiritual wellbeing. This capacity is one of the many gifts from God; understanding and correctly utilizing the gift is our responsibility. I have sometimes used the analogy of the various lights and signals on the dashboard of a car to describe feelings. The dashboard lights and gauges were installed to help me, the driver, properly attend to the information they communicate. Refusing to identify and responsibly attend to my feelings is the equivalent of covering up the dashboard in the belief that "what I don't know won't hurt me." Obviously, any number of outcomes, ranging from the annoying to the catastrophic, can be the result of totally ignoring the dashboard's "messages." When extending this metaphor to feelings, ignoring them is the equivalent of a person saying, "I'm numb, as I don't feel anything" — which I have often heard in workshops or therapy sessions. I generally respond to these statements by saying "numbness" is not a Family of Feelings; it's a refusal to acknowledge and identify one's feelings.

Back to the metaphorical dashboard: if the gauge is showing that I am low on fuel, my refusal to respond to this information will predictably result in me having to spend more time, energy, and money to remedy the situation when the vehicle comes to a halt; I may be inviting additional danger to myself as well, depending on when and where I run out of gas. Similarly, prolonged periods of "parking in numbness" will create havoc in the physical, mental, emotional, and spiritual life of the individual as well as that of their friends and family.

In addition to the dangers of emotional "numbness," there are other harmful implications and results of gender-based, culturally ascribed feelings. So, if the culturally sanctioned primary Family of Feelings for males is Mad, then a man who is feeling Sad or Scared is likely to ignore and dismiss these feelings, instead blowing off steam through anger, the only valve available to him. If he is feeling Sad, which means he is in need of time and space to grieve a loss and to seek nurturance, he is unlikely to get these needs met by expressing anger; the recipient of his anger will more likely retaliate by expressing his or her own anger. Similarly, if he is feeling Scared, he needs protection — but expressing anger will probably not help him get it.

If the metaphorical dashboard light comes on to indicate that I am "low on oil," but I keep putting water in the radiator or topping off the gas tank, I may be under the illusion that I am attending to the car — but since I have not correctly identified the problem, my attempted solutions are ineffectual, leading to increasingly serious outcomes that could include a burnt transmission. If that happens, a problem that could have been quickly corrected at minimal expense would then become a major drain on my time, energy, and resources.

This culturally imposed lack of permission to acknowledge and express certain Families of Feelings for each gender results in what a brilliant friend and colleague, Wekesa O. Madzimoyo, has called "substitution patterns." Even though culturally sanctioned Families of Feelings are harmful for both genders, the burden is heavier for males, since out of the four Families of Feelings they only have Mad and (to some extent) Glad available to them. This means that two entire Families of Feelings, or two mission-critical dashboard lights, are routinely and habitually ignored and suppressed, which takes a heavy toll on men's health and longevity, and has deleterious effects on their intimate relationships.

Culturally, women are given sanction to feel and express more of their feelings, since Mad is the only taboo Family. Unfortunately, discouraging the expression of anger works against women as well. In a situation where a woman needs to stand her ground and set or reset her boundaries because her rights have been violated, she may scare herself out of a confrontation altogether, or in the confrontation process she may burst into tears and substitute Sad for Mad. With either substitution pattern, her needs go unmet. When she swaps Scared for Mad, she doesn't address her real feeling; and when she replaces Mad with Sad, she might get a response such as "There, there, don't cry" and some unwelcome, ineffectual comforting that will leave her more frustrated and powerless. She has thus inadvertently participated in victimizing herself by manifesting culturally prescribed patterns of behavior.

Our Creator (in the Owner's Manual) has never ascribed gender-based expression of feelings. Nothing in our creation is random; any inherent or potential capacity has its own specific function and purpose. In the same way that a car's dashboard gauges and lights are placed there to enable the driver to properly maintain the car, our God-given capacity to feel has the specific function of enabling us to safeguard our wellbeing.

Since both our ability to think and to feel have been given to us by our Creator, I believe that the soundest decisions are reached when we take both our feelings and our thinking into account. Decisions based only on one or the other—my cognition or my emotions—are equally inadequate, because I have left out a necessary part of the equation.

Sometimes, in multicultural training workshops, we would get questions from a participant around a concept we had shared. No matter how many explanations we would offer, this person would continue saying, "But I am still confused." It would become clear to us that the resulting confusion was based on his refusal to deal with an underlying prejudicial feeling of which he might not be entirely aware—but, as an astute colleague from VISIONS was fond of saying, "There are no thinking solutions to feeling problems."

We Bahá'ís have been blessed not only with an ocean of information and guidance relative to this earthly life and the one to come, we have also been gifted with the person of 'Abdu'l-Bahá as our Exemplar; he alone exemplified to perfection every principle and commandment of Bahá'u'lláh. By His very being, as well as through His Writings, Talks and even the most casual contact with any human being, he reflected all the divine virtues and attributes of God. If we wish to know about the enactment of love, justice, mercy and other innumerable virtues and attributes, we can find hundreds of examples by studying the life and Writings of 'Abdu'l-Bahá.

Having said that, attempting to emulate 'Abdu'l-Bahá in my daily life could easily drive me to despair, because I would find in myself nothing but flaws and shortcomings. If that threatens to happen, I need to remind myself of the love, patience, and kindness with which He guided the development of each soul who had the bounty of being in His presence. He certainly would not want me to be so discouraged that I would quit trying altogether; in fact, in response to an individual who requested guidance about her own spiritual growth and transformation, 'Abdu'l-Bahá's succinct reply was "Little by little, day by day" (in *The Bahá'í World Vol. 12*, 706). Within this brief reply is an ocean of wisdom and guidance. Psychotherapeutic theory and practice firmly supports the reality that behavioral change is an incremental and evolutionary process, and that progress starts with taking continuous little steps: "Little by little, day by day." Similarly, the two things that we need to know about spiritual growth can be summed up in the words "begin" and "continue."

For me, as a Bahá'í and a therapist, the greatest joy has been to find parallels between the theory and practice of psychotherapy and the Divine Guidance of the Writings, affirming the principle of harmony between science and religion. My process, as I am sure with any Bahá'í in his or her particular profession, has been to seek supporting guidance in the Writings for any proposed theory or practice; my study and practice of "Feelings as Messengers" was no exception. I once developed a course entitled "Being Happy, A Delectable Duty"; this information appears in a later chapter of this book. The inspiration for this course was 'Abdu'l-Bahá's insistence on the importance of joy and happiness, given His characteristic inquiry upon meeting an individual: "Are you happy?" 'Abdu'l-Bahá is quoted in *Star of the West* as saying, "The soul of man must be happy no matter where he is. One must attain to the condition of inward beatitude and peace, then outward circumstances will not alter his spiritual calmness and joyousness" (*Vol. 1*, 161).

This quote led me to wonder about 'Abdu'l-Bahá's expression of the other emotions of the Family of Feelings. To my delight, I found many vignettes in which our Perfect Exemplar fully and vigorously not only felt, but openly expressed, His range of feelings. Above all, the Master lived in the Glad family of feelings and freely expressed all its shades of joyful, peaceful, and powerful. Even in his years of incarceration and exile, He brought joy to others with his superb sense of humor by constantly reminding them that happiness was a spiritual state that one should choose to live in, often in spite of one's external life conditions. By no means did this mean that He ignored His other feelings; there are numerous accounts of 'Abdu'l-Bahá expressing sadness by weeping openly when news of the persecution or martyrdom of Persian friends reached Him. During His journey in the United States, whenever He was surrounded by magnificent natural surroundings, 'Abdu'l-Bahá expressed deep sadness for His beloved father, Bahá'u'lláh, Who had been through long periods of incarceration and deprived of His much beloved natural settings.

When 'Abdu'l-Bahá first read the following prayer revealed by Bahá'u'lláh during His sojourn in Sulamáníyyih, He said, "When for the first time I read this Tablet, I wept openly" (Dr. Zia Baghdádí, as cited in Furútan, *Stories of Bahá'u'lláh*, 20).

> Create in me a pure heart, O My God, and renew a tranquil conscience within me, O my Hope! Through the spirit of power confirm Thou me in Thy Cause, O my Best-Beloved, and by the light of Thy glory reveal unto me Thy path, O Thou the Goal of my desire! Through the power of Thy transcendent might lift me up unto the heaven of Thy holiness, O Source of my being, and by the breezes of Thine eternity gladden me, O Thou Who art my God! Let Thine everlasting melodies breathe tranquility on me, O my Companion, and let the riches of Thine ancient countenance deliver me from all except Thee, O my Master, and let the tidings of the revelation of Thine Incorruptible Essence bring me joy, O Thou Who art the most manifest of the manifest and the most hidden of the hidden! (Bahá'u'lláh, in *Bahá'í Prayers*, 162)

There is also the poignant account of Him interring the sacred remains of the Báb:

> When all was finished, and the earthly remains of the Martyr-Prophet of Shíráz were, at long last, safely deposited for their everlasting rest in the bosom of God's holy mountain, `Abdu'l-Bahá, Who had cast aside His turban, removed His shoes and thrown off His cloak, bent low over the still open sarcophagus, His silver hair waving about His head and His face transfigured and luminous, rested His forehead on the border of the wooden casket, and, sobbing aloud, wept with such a weeping that all those who were present wept with Him. That night He could not sleep, so overwhelmed was He with emotion. (Shoghi Effendi, *God Passes By*, 276)

When it comes to the Family of Mad, there is much guidance in the Writings and many admonitions about its proper and improper expressions. We will start with a few examples about the dangerous implications and impact of its improper use.

Jealousy consumeth the body and anger doth burn the liver, avoid these two as you would a lion.
(Bahá'u'lláh, in Universal House of Justice,
Compilation of Compilations, Vol. 1, 460)

...the tongue is a smoldering fire, and excess of speech a deadly poison. Material fire consumeth the body, whereas the fire of the tongue devoureth both heart and soul. The force of the former lasteth but for a time, whilst the effects of the latter endureth a century.
(Bahá'u'lláh, Gleanings, 265)

...distinguish one's self through good deeds...not to lose one's temper.
(Bahá'u'lláh, Kitáb-i-Aqdas, 49–50)

...if he cometh upon wrath he shall manifest love.
(Bahá'u'lláh, The Seven Valleys, 1)

The individual must be educated to such a high degree that he...would think it easier to be slashed with a sword or pierced with a spear than to utter calumny or be carried away by wrath.
('Abdu'l-Bahá, Selections, 136)

Never become angry with one another....Love the creatures for the sake of God and of for themselves. You will never become angry or impatient if you love them for the sake of God.
('Abdu'l-Bahá, Promulgation of Universal Peace, 93)

Naturally, following the above guidance and admonitions might feel impossible and overwhelming. However, as with significant parts of the overarching spiritual guidance found the Writings, we must remind ourselves that these are lifelong aspirational goals. Just as when we practice other virtues, we will often engage in a continuous process of trial and error in our attempts to modify our behavior and bring it into closer alignment with the high standards put forth in the Writings. In my opinion, the goal is not to deny anger when we feel it; the goal is to train ourselves in its proper use. 'Abdu'l-Bahá advocated that anger can be useful because it is the correct response to injustice: "If he exercises his anger and wrath against the bloodthirsty tyrants who are like ferocious beasts it is most praiseworthy; but if he does not use these qualities in a right way, they would be blameworthy" ('Abdu'l-Bahá, in *Bahá'í World Faith*, 320).

To reinforce this point, I offer a few accounts of 'Abdu'l-Bahá demonstrating through His example the correct course of action, even when a situation provoked anger. He stood firm against even the smallest injustice, as his refusal to pay the extra and unearned money to the driver of the cab or carriage shows. Rúhíyyih Khánum (Rúhíyyih Rabbání) wrote:

> Shoghi Effendi said that one day he was driving back from Alexandria to Ramleh with the Master in a rented carriage, accompanied by a Pasha who was going to the Master's house as His guest; when they arrived and got out the Master asked the strapping big coachman how much He owed him the man asked an exorbitant price; 'Abdu'l-Bahá refused to pay it, the man insisted and became abusive to such an extent that he grasped the Master by the sash around His waist and pulled Him roughly back and forth, insisting on this price. Shoghi Effendi said this scene in front of the distinguished guest embarrassed him terribly. He was too small to do anything himself to help the Master and felt horrified and humiliated. Not so 'Abdu'l-Bahá, Who remained perfectly calm and refused to give in. When the man finally released his hold, the Master paid him exactly what He owed him, told him his conduct had forfeited the good tip He had planned to give him, and walked off followed by Shoghi Effendi and the Pasha! There is no doubt that such things left a lifelong imprint on the Guardian's character, who never allowed himself to be browbeaten or cheated, no matter whether or not this embarrassed or inconvenienced him, and those who were working for him. (*The Priceless Pearl*, 23)

Dr. Yúnis Khán Afrúkhtih, a highly devoted Persian Bahá'í, lived in 'Akká for nine years and often served as 'Abdu'l-Bahá's translator and secretary. He wrote a memoir that recorded some of his keen observations of the Master's attitudes and interactions with the numerous daily Bahá'í and non-Bahá'í visitors, which were always aimed at the training of souls. He asserted that "the mere glance of 'Abdu'l-Bahá upon a believer released mysterious forces which at times were capable of transforming his life." Among the summary of his observations describing the various effects of the Master's glances is the following one about anger:

> One glance, which thankfully did not appear except on rare occasions, was that of wrath and anger. It reflected the wrath of God from which one had to flee for refuge to Him… (*Khátirát-i-Nuh-Sálih* [Memoirs of Nine Years], 570–73)

There is also a pilgrim's account cited in the book *Vignettes from the Life of 'Abdu'l-Bahá*, compiled and edited by Annamarie Honnold:

> Soon after the arrival of Bahá'u'lláh and his party in 'Akká, the governor visited the barracks for inspection. 'Abdu'l-Bahá, accompanied by a

few believers, went to see him. But the Governor was discourteous and spoke to them in a provocative manner. He threatened to cut the supply of bread if one of the prisoners went missing and then ordered them back to their room. One of the Master's attendants could not bear to remain silent after such insulting treatment. He retorted with rage and hurled back at the governor some offensive remarks. 'Abdu'l-Bahá immediately chastened his attendant by slapping him hard in the face in front of the Governor and ordering him to return to his room. This action by 'Abdu'l-Bahá not only diffused a dangerous situation, but also opened the eyes of the Governor to the existence of a real leader among the prisoners, a leader who would act with authority and justice. Due to this action the Governor's attitude toward 'Abdu'l-Bahá changed. He realized that contrary to the wild rumors in 'Akká at the time, 'Abdu'l-Bahá and his family were from a noble background and not criminals as he had been led to believe. The Governor therefore began to act in a more humane way towards the prisoners. He allowed a small part of the prisoners, escorted by guards, to visit the markets of 'Akká daily to buy their provisions. (47)

In the above example, the servant's behavior was a demonstration of an impulsive angry reaction that could have exacerbated the plight of the prisoners; 'Abdu'l-Bahá's necessary chastisement, born out of wisdom, diffused this potentially dangerous situation. To me, these accounts demonstrate that although 'Abdu'l-Bahá at times may have felt anger, He never impulsively reacted to it. His actions always provided informative and instructive models of behavior for us, regardless of situation.

When considering the Scared feelings family, it is helpful to recall that the Writings generally encourage us to diminish or overcome our fears by increasing our trust in a loving God.

Be not afraid of anyone, place thy whole trust in God, the Almighty, the All-knowing.

(Bahá'u'lláh, *Tablets of Bahá'u'lláh*, 190)

O Son of Man! Thou art My dominion and My dominion perisheth not, wherefore fearest thou thy perishing?...Abide then in thy love for Me, that thou mayest find Me in the realms of glory.

(Bahá'u'lláh, *Hidden Words*, 7)

Were men to discover the motivating purpose of God's Revelation, they would assuredly cast away their fears, and with hearts filled with gratitude, rejoice with exceeding gladness.

(Bahá'u'lláh, *Gleanings*, 175)

I give praise to Thee, O my God....Thou art He Who changeth through His bidding abasement into glory, and weakness into strength, and powerlessness into might, and fear into calm, and doubt into certainty.

(Bahá'u'lláh, *Bahá'í Prayers*, 122–23)

'Abdu'l-Bahá, our Exemplar, never expressed fear for Himself. His fear was at the universal level, for what would befall humanity as it turned its back on God and followed the dictates of its lower nature. He warned people about the coming of a world war early in the 20th century, before the notion of a world war even existed. At a more personal and community level, He expressed fear or concern about various individuals' firmness in the Covenant. He was constantly concerned about our spiritual development and He prayed earnestly that individual Bahá'ís would comprehend and emphasize their essential spiritual nature instead of focusing primarily or exclusively on their physical and material wellbeing.

It is important to remember, however, 'Abdu'l-Bahá's emphasis on the importance of Glad. In Earl Redman's book *'Abdu'l-Bahá in Their Midst*, 'Abdu'l-Bahá spoke to a believer about the power of happiness, saying, "One must often bring serious discussions through jokes, and then they will give happiness and rejoicing. Some people have frowns and are always serious. This is because of the narrowness of their thoughts. All should be open-hearted and smiling" (160).

This cursory examination of our Exemplar's ever-present insistence of dwelling in joy and happiness, and his free and often public expression of a rich array of diverse feelings, makes me think of this particular diagram about FAM (Figure 14, next page).

This diagram is one of my favorites, because I see it as most compatible with my limited understanding of guidance from the Writings of Bahá'u'lláh and 'Abdu'l-Bahá and the myriad examples offered in the conduct of 'Abdu'l-Bahá, whom we are to emulate. Glad encompasses the top three segments: Powerful, Joyful, and Peaceful.

What I glean from 'Abdu'l-Bahá's modeling and His Writings is that true happiness is a spiritual phenomenon based not on the external events of my life, which are at best temporary, but almost in *spite* of them. True happiness is a spiritual condition. I need to truly understand that I have been created by a loving God who wants me to love Him back, as Bahá'u'lláh has written in *The Hidden Words*: "Love Me that I may love thee" (4). He has indeed sent an updated "Owner's Manual" (through His Messenger Bahá'u'lláh) with all the guidance I need to fulfill the very purpose of my creation, which Bahá'u'lláh reveals in the Short Obligatory prayer: "I bear witness O my God that Thou hast created me to know Thee and to worship

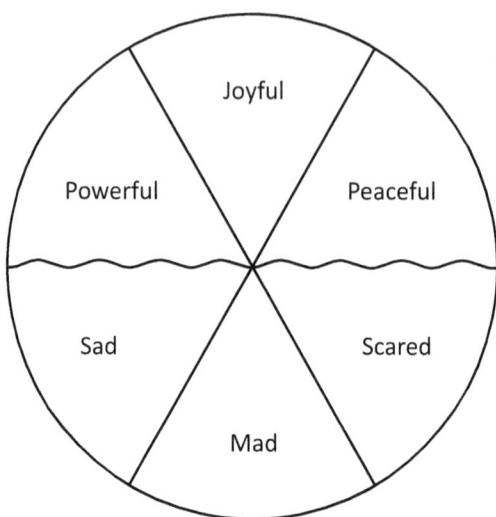

Figure 14. Another way of depicting the Family of Feelings. Information adapted from VISIONS training materials: Reprinted with permission from VISIONS Inc.

Thee..." (*Bahá'í Prayers*, 4). God defines Himself as an unknowable essence, yet He allows us to know Him through the Intermediaries chosen by Him, Who are the embodiments of all the qualities and attributes of God. These Intermediaries are the purest channels conveying the Holy Spirit of God. This, briefly and inadequately put, is the "knowing" part. The "loving" part is my lifelong, continuous efforts to follow and obey the guidelines He has put forth that will lead me to my happiness. "Think not that We have revealed unto you a mere code of laws. Nay, rather, We have unsealed the choice Wine with the fingers of might and power" (Bahá'u'lláh, *Gleanings*, 332). As 'Abdu'l-Bahá states, "no happiness is sweeter than spiritual comprehension of the Divine Teachings" (*Promulgation of Universal Peace*, 460).

It is a challenging balancing act, in which I must acknowledge and responsibly meet the needs of my physical material self without losing sight of the fact that I am meant to be primarily a spiritual being; only through the comprehension of this reality can I truly be happy. It is not that I should not enjoy my physical/material side – in fact, he urges me to do just that. As Bahá'u'lláh writes,

> *Should a man wish to adorn himself with the ornaments of the earth, to wear its apparels, or partake of the benefits it can bestow, no harm can befall him, if*

he alloweth nothing whatever to intervene between him and God, for God hath ordained every good thing, whether created in the heavens or in the earth, for such of His servants that truly believe in Him. Eat ye, O people, of the good things which God hath allowed you, and deprive not yourselves from His wondrous bounties. Render thanks and praise unto Him, and be of them that are truly thankful. (Gleanings, 276)

However, He also instructs and warns me that these joys are limited and temporary. If I over-focus on meeting my physical needs and wants, I will have missed out on the most important purpose of my life, which is developing my spiritual qualities and attributes. In fact, our Creator wants this development for all for us.

The honor of the human kingdom is the attainment of spiritual happiness in the human world, the acquisition of the knowledge and love of God…if material happiness and spiritual felicity be conjoined, it will be "delight upon delight" as the Arabs say.

('Abdu'l-Bahá, *Promulgation of Universal Peace*, 166)

Man is, in reality, a spiritual being, and only when he lives in the spirit is he truly happy.

('Abdu'l-Bahá, *Paris Talks*, 72)

Spiritual enjoyment brings always joy. The love of God brings endless happiness. These are joys in themselves and not alleviations.

('Abdu'l-Bahá, *Paris Talks*, 111)

Peace of mind is gained by the centering of the spiritual consciousness on the Prophet of God; therefore you should study the spiritual Teachings and receive the Water of Life from the holy Utterances. Then by translating these high ideals into action, your entire character will be changed, and your mind will not only find peace, but your entire being will find joy and enthusiasm.

(letter written on behalf of the Guardian, in Hornby, *Lights of Guidance*, 112)

Then it is clear that the honour and exaltation of man cannot reside solely in material delights and earthly benefits. This material felicity is wholly secondary, while the exaltation of man resides primarily in such virtues and attainments as are the adornments of the human reality.

('Abdu'l-Bahá, *Some Answered Questions*, 79)

When we look at the diagram (Figure 14), we can say that essentially 'Abdu'l-Bahá repeatedly instructed us to "park" in the three top realms of the Glad zone.

> *A happy state brings special blessings. When the mind is depressed, the blessings are not received. Laugh and talk, don't lament and talk. Laugh and speak. Laughter is caused by the slackening or relaxation of the nerves. It is an ideal condition and not physical. Laughter is the visible effect of an invisible cause. For example, happiness and misery are super-sensuous phenomena. One cannot hear them with his ears or touch them with his hands. Happiness is a spiritual state.*
>
> ('Abdu'l-Bahá, *Star of the West*, Vol. 13, 102)

> *The Blessed Beauty often remarked: "There are four qualities which I love to see manifested in people: First, enthusiasm and courage; Second, a face wreathed in smiles and a radiant countenance; Third, that they see all things with their own eyes and not through the eyes of others; Fourth, the ability to carry a task, once begun, through to its end.*
>
> (Dr. Zia Baghdádí, as cited in Furútan, *Stories of Bahá'u'lláh*, 51)

All of these admonishments about being happy were not in denial of our other feelings—just the opposite. When we observe His behavior, we see His model: He acknowledged all feelings, took corrective action, and returned to the magnificent Glad zone (our spiritual reality). As with the example of the car, we ought to be functioning at our optimum level in the Glad zone, with its message of "All is well, keep on keeping on." The only way to remain in the Glad zone is by attending to the cautionary messages sent from our dashboard lights—from Mad, Sad, and Scared feelings—so we can once again return to the state of inner joy, peace, and power. The responsibility is ours.

If I do not understand my spiritual development and ignore it, this course of action is like going against the instructions provided my car's owner's manual. There will be consequences—not to the car manufacturer, but to me, the owner and user. By ignoring the "Owner's Manual" for my life, however, I live in denial that what separates me from the animal kingdom is my soul, my intellect, and the fact that I have been gifted with the freedom of choice. Of course, the freedom to choose is a tricky gift; the good news here is that I'm in charge, and the bad news is that I'm in charge. ☺ Animals have no choice but to follow the dictates of their instincts to eat, sleep, procreate, and, within their limited capacity, "enjoy" their existence (that is, if we humans let them!). Since animals have not been given the gift or "curse" of choice, they are content within the confines of their material existence. As a human being, however, if I primarily pursue the needs and the endless wants of my physical side, I will end up empty, unfulfilled, exhausted, and frustrated, asking a version of the question "Is that all there is?" No—but that is all I chose to pursue.

As I have attempted to take more and more responsibility for my overall wellbeing, I have found the following statement from my late beloved trainer/therapist Jo Lewis very helpful: "As adults we are 100% responsible for the intensity and the duration of any feeling in response to internal or external stimuli." At first, this statement sounds daunting and burdensome, but in practice I have found it to be empowering and freeing. It reminds me that I get to decide how intensely and for how long I will experience a certain emotional response.

Many years ago, I witnessed the truth of the above statement, or rather, the result of not following it. My mother and I were guests at a wedding reception, and as is often the case, we were seated at a table with another family that we did not know. The lady of the family was clad in black and the mood was rather somber. As we introduced ourselves and started sharing information about our lives, she mournfully reported the loss of one of her sons; her other son was present at the table. The intensity of her emotions was such that I was sure that the death had occurred quite recently, but further conversation revealed that the son had died over ten years ago. This stance is likely to be based on a belief such as "You never recover from the loss of a child and will be in constant intense agony for the rest of your life." Of course, it is true that there is no correct or universal pattern for grieving and each individual may do it differently. However, if I am ruled by the above belief, it will become a self-fulfilling prophecy. I felt saddened for the rest of her family, especially the other son, who had to live under the shadow of this intense, prolonged grief.

It is my sincere hope that the section on Feelings as Messengers has powerfully demonstrated the vital need to improve our abilities to both accurately identify and take corrective action on our various feelings, as they are major components of self-care and empowerment

Strokes: Emotional Fuel for Life

Eric Berne, the founder of Transactional Analysis, defined a stroke as "a basic unit of recognition" (in James and Jongeward, *Born to Win*, 44). If I look at someone and smile at them, I am basically recognizing their "being." In the Zulu language, the word for "hello" is "I see you," which is a lovely way of recognizing and acknowledging another human being. Strokes can take the form of an actual physical touch as well as verbal or non-verbal forms of recognition, such as a nod, a smile, or a waving of a hand.

They could even be considered emotional fuel for life because strokes are *essential* for our survival. They are not a luxury; they are an absolute necessity! Berne identified certain basic hungers that are universally experienced; one of these he described as hunger for physical and mental stimulation, which he called "stimulus hunger." This primal need for attention and affection has been highlighted through several animal and human infant experiments (e.g., Spitz, "Hospitalism," 53–74). In Spitz's study, the infants in an orphanage were divided into two groups; all matters, such as feeding schedules, physical conditions of the room, diaper changing, and the like, were the same. The only difference between the two groups was that in one, only the physical needs of the infants were met without any other stimuli, while in the other group volunteers came to interact, touch, and hold the babies at regular intervals. After a period of 4 to 6 months, they observed a phenomenal difference in the condition of the children in the two groups: the babies in the first group lagged behind in their physical development. The differences in overall wellbeing among the infants in both groups was equally dramatic; those in the first group were withdrawn and showed little interest in their environment. Some of the babies were so severely affected that they died at the end of six months. This unfortunate and astounding outcome graphically demonstrates that our need for interaction, attention, and affection is at the cellular level.

Among Transactional analysts there is a saying: "If the infant is not stroked, his spinal cord shrivels up" (James and Jongeward, *Born to Win*, 45).

I learned in my training that in some ancient cultures, the severest form of punishment was that on a designated day and time, all the members of a tribe would start completely ignoring the offending person as if he or she simply did not exist—the very opposite of the "I see you" greeting. The impact of this punishment must have been devastating.

In the first months of life, the infant thrives by being held, touched, spoken to, and the countless ways in which parents welcome a baby into its new life. Berne's use of the word "stroke" was based on the need of infants to be held and touched. As we grow older, our need for physical touch (strokes) does not diminish, but we expand the shapes and forms strokes can take to better fulfill that need—they can be a pat on the back for a job well done, a verbal compliment, or a check received for our work.

What we do with strokes for adults, both in giving and receiving them, goes back to those crucial first years of life. Once again, the child is an experimental scientist: highly motivated by his innate instinct to survive and strive, he constantly observes the behaviors of the parents toward each other, himself, and/or other siblings. Given that we seem to be innately aware of our need for attention and recognition, we are constantly keeping track of who gets noticed in our family of origin, how they get noticed, and for what reason. On the basis of this ongoing observation, we draw conclusions about what we need to do in order to get noticed and gain our parents' or caregivers' attention. If we are blessed to be in a loving, supportive, and praising family, we learn to be okay in our own skin; we develop a basic sense of "OK-ness" that says, "I am worthy of a measure of attention and affection just because I exist." This sense is an example of unconditional love: "I am loved because I am; I don't have to do anything to earn this love."

We also learn that there is such a thing as "conditional love," or strokes. For instance, when I did certain things as a child, I seemed to please my parents, who showed their approval in a variety of ways—a verbal phrase, a smile, or another reward. When I did certain other things, I still won their attention, but then I might get "negative strokes," such as a frown or another sign of displeasure. Once a pattern is established, I would tend to repeat the actions that yield the greatest amount of attention.

In a healthy family, there would be an abundance of unconditional positive "being" strokes, balanced by some conditional positive and negative "doing" strokes. If there is an overabundance of "being" strokes and not many positive and/or negative "doing" strokes to help shape my behavior, I may develop a false sense of entitlement (e.g., "I don't have to do much of anything" or "The world owes me just because I am") or a sense of powerlessness ("My actions seem to have no impact or effect"). Neither outcome will serve me well later in life. If, on the other hand, I don't get enough "being" strokes but plenty of "doing" strokes, I might tend to struggle as an adult to do more and more, always trying to earn my strokes — and unaware that I deserve some strokes just for being.

There is no redeeming value in unconditional negative strokes. They are poisonous, because they imply that the child's very being is wrong, and there's nothing to be done about it. Attributions such as "you are stupid" (unconditional negative stroke) instead of "that behavior was stupid" (conditional negative stroke) strike a child at the core of their being, and do not provide them with guidance to modify or shape their behavior. Ironically, since the child's task is always to please the parents, they take attributions such as "you are bad" or "you are worthless" as definition of self, which they then proceed to fulfill.

It is crucial to remember that the most harmful condition is total lack of attention. Our innate and vital need to be noticed is so deep that it seems as if we are saying, "You notice me, therefore I am." Being totally ignored, therefore, can be potentially more harmful than receiving negative attention. Let's imagine a family sitting at the dinner table in a silent, glum atmosphere where a child feels invisible and ignored. It is understandable that out of that instinctual need for being noticed, the child might "accidentally" knock over his milk or water glass, knowing full well that he may receive a verbal chastisement, a name-calling, or even physical punishment, depending on the family's level of dysfunction. The child, however, seems to be programmed to know that even the worst form of negative attention is more life enhancing than no attention at all.

VISIONS developed this helpful figure to summarize the types of strokes. Figure 15 also outlines the five things we can do to promote a healthy "stroke economy" for ourselves and for others.

As humans, we need a good dose of positive and negative conditional "doing" strokes; they help shape our character by making us aware of the effects of our behavior on others. Certain behaviors are met with approval and bring children many forms of positive strokes: "Good girl [or boy], you did such a good job of cleaning your plate"; "I am proud of how you put your toys away"; or "You are so good at sharing your cookies with your friend."

Negative conditional strokes are equally important in shaping and modifying our behavior. In this context, "negative" does not connote "bad or deficient." For instance, I might have accidentally knocked over my peas and carrots from my high chair once or twice, which didn't seem to please

The Stroke Economy

Stroke = Unit of Recognition

	Positive	Negative
Doing (Conditional)	"Great job." "You really pulled that one out." "Here is your paycheck."	"You didn't get that report in on time." "Don't park in my driveway, stupid."
Being (Unconditional)	"Hello." "I like your style." "You are beautiful." "I love you."	"Gee, I'm stupid." "Drop dead." "I wish you were never born."

Stroke Economy:
We do FIVE things with strokes:

1. Give strokes
2. Receive strokes
3. Reject strokes
4. Ask for strokes
5. Self-stroke

Figure 15. The Stroke Economy. In a healthy environment we can do all of the above freely. However, there are myths that we grew up with that constrict and direct our personal use of strokes. Information adapted from VISIONS training materials. Reprinted with permission from VISIONS Inc.

Mother at all. However, given that I am a little scientist at work, I may decide to—intentionally—throw my food just to see what happens. Naturally, my behavior is met with a greater level of disapproval, drawing more negative attention or strokes. Through a myriad of repetitions, I learn that certain behaviors are not good and should therefore be avoided. Although we need both positive and negative "doing" strokes in the formation of our character, as well as in the process of formulating a provisional answer to the third Basic Question of "How do I make it in the world," it is generally agreed that a greater measure of positive "being" and "doing" strokes is necessary for the formation of a healthy, well-balanced person.

Claude Steiner, a well-known theoretician, author, and practitioner in Transactional Analysis circles, has highlighted the formation of stroking patterns learned in infancy and childhood by the term "stroke economy" (Steiner, "The Stroke Economy," 9–15). Children come away with their own conclusions about strokes, and this conclusion is dependent on the family of origin's level of emotional/psychological health—and according to Steiner, most of what they learn is not conducive to healthy living. He believed that parents, in or out of awareness, put the following restrictions on strokes:

- don't give strokes when you have them to give
- don't ask for strokes when you need them
- don't accept strokes if you want them
- don't reject strokes when you don't want them
- don't give yourself strokes

Of course, not all families would prescribe such a stark set of prohibitions; however, in practice, most of us can find some degree of these restrictions in operation. As with all the other messages we swallowed whole as children, we tend to follow the patterns of the stroke economy put in place by our family. We behave as if these restrictions are truth and reality, unaware that they were two imperfect individuals' perceptions of reality. As a result, most of us may live our lives in varying degrees of "stroke deprivation." Considering that as an adult I am 100% responsible for my overall wellbeing 100% of the time, it behooves me to examine carefully my inheritance relative to stroke economy. This consideration will help me free myself from any erroneous misconceptions and restrictions, in addition to being an independent investigation of truth.

Now, I can update the pattern of my stroke economy, using the assumption of "abundance" rather than "scarcity." There are five elements that I can address and update to enhance my internal and external stroke economy.

1. Give
2. Receive
3. Reject
4. Ask for
5. Self-stroke

In giving a stroke, I should offer only what I truly feel; to give a stroke that is not heartfelt and authentic is like giving someone a plastic rose, void of natural beauty and fragrance. I may also have to overcome a restrictive notion that if I give out too many strokes, I may run out of them. In my own experience, the more I practiced giving authentic strokes, the more adept I became in actually recognizing praiseworthy attributes in others. There truly is no scarcity! I can develop sensitivity around the appropriate time and place to offer my strokes, too.

When it comes to receiving a stroke, most of us have barriers based on the "stroke economy" of our family of origin, in addition to ones that stem from our religious and cultural heritage. In our head, we may revisit sayings such as "Don't get a swelled head"; "They're just flattering me — they don't mean it"; "I wonder what they want in return"; or "If they knew the real me, they wouldn't give me this stroke." If we think of strokes as the "emotional fuel for life" or the rays of sunlight all life needs, we each have our individual "protective" shields that keep us from taking in these life-enhancing offerings. We know whether we have truly taken in a stroke by experiencing a sense of wellbeing, a sense of being truly seen by someone else in that moment.

Based on our experiences in childhood, some of us have a lot more to overcome than others. I remember, in my days as a novice therapist over 30 years ago, being shocked by the reaction of a therapy group member. When offered a stroke, she would show signs of great distress and almost get panicky; I had never before seen such a response to an offered stroke. Upon further exploration, she revealed that as a little girl she had been the object of much unwanted and inappropriate attention from her stepfather and his friends, which of course left her confused, frightened, and helpless. She had lived with these feelings for over 30 years, so she had to learn anew that not all verbal or physical strokes were inappropriate or invasive, and that as an adult she deserved to receive these life-enhancing offerings — if and when she wanted them.

There are some strokes that are not complimentary, or, at best, present a confusing mixed message. A classic example could be meeting up with a person after several years to hear them say something like, "Wow, ___ you look so much better!" They're smiling as they say this and it sounds like they are giving you a stroke, but you are left with questions like "I look better than what or whom?" or "I wonder how I looked to them before." Typically, we may spend a great deal of time trying to analyze or understand this "stroke." The healthy thing to do is to let it roll off our back and simply reject it.

When it comes to asking for the strokes we want, we have to overcome many cultural myths, such as "If you have to ask for it, it's no good!" or "If you ask for it, the response is not real!" This stance implies that others should be able to read our mind, accurately determine our wants, and present them to us without any of our input. Some people also confuse "asking" with "begging," and feel that it would put them in a "one down" position. Others scare themselves by thinking, "What if I ask for it and the person refuses to give me the requested stroke?" These are inherited or self-made barriers. The truth is that in asking for a stroke I want, my request come from my empowered position as an adult who has taken full responsibility for her own wellbeing. I also know that even if I am refused the stroke, I will still be quite okay in that I have stood up for myself. Naturally, there is vulnerability in asking for what we want, but this vulnerability should not be mistaken for weakness. To me, weakness lies in not doing anything on my own behalf, not identifying for myself what strokes I want, and passively waiting for the other person to correctly guess what I want and offer it to me.

The final input I can have in managing my "stroke economy" is self-stroking. Many of us seem to depend mostly on external strokes, but ironically, the "self" is the only source that is available to us from cradle to grave. In fact, I believe that the more generous I am by inwardly and authentically giving myself strokes (not to be confused with feeding my ego), the more inclined I am to be generous and authentic in the strokes I offer to others. After all, none of us can give what we don't have. I also see here an application of the saying "charity begins at home." There are times when only I can fully appreciate an accomplishment, because only I know my own journey. Let's say I read a passage from the Writings at a gathering; for most people, this would not stand out as a praiseworthy act. But knowing my own history of having been petrified to say more than two words publicly, I would be more than justified to celebrate my progress and offer myself many strokes, which would encourage me to take further steps to overcome more self- or other-imposed limitations. If inwardly I am stingy with my self-strokes, I am likely to go through life in a state of "stroke deprivation" and develop an unhealthy dependence on strokes from others.

Now, we turn to some of the Transactional Analysis theory that I have found particularly useful when it comes to translating this supreme law of love into actions toward myself and others. What I have observed, relative to taking adult responsibility for our own wellbeing and being "fair unto ourselves," is that we can create a lot of problems for ourselves and others when we relinquish this responsibility. When I am not upfront with my "stroke" needs and wants because (1) I have not even bothered to identify them for myself, probably in the name of "forgetting the self" or (2) I don't feel that it is legitimate for me to acknowledge these needs and wants,

I will tend to meet these needs crookedly. Rather than acknowledging where I am on my journey toward wholeness, I may pretend that I have already attained a position of not needing any strokes. I have found this pretend stance of "humility" to be highly dysfunctional. This is not to say that the individual is necessarily being deceitful; it could be that they are trying to practice the virtue of humility. If they continue on this path of self-unawareness, however, they cannot realistically make progress. This person could also become a source of contention and disunity within a community; if a person is conflicted and not unified within themselves, they cannot manifest harmony and unity toward others—or, at the very least, their offerings will not have the potency of a congruent and authentic self.

In order to tie this discussion to the ways in which this "stroke" theory has worked in my own life, I must acknowledge that at first, I felt awkward and somewhat conflicted. In my then-perception of the five things one should do to improve one's own "stroke economy," only the first one, that of offering strokes, seemed congruent with the Writings. However, as I gradually made efforts to practice the other four things, and through my later observations of their impact on my group members, I concluded that there was essential harmony between the Writings and these practices as tools.

Learning to accept and receive genuine strokes from others didn't give me a big head; instead, it served as a balm to my soul. At first with awkwardness and incredulity and, later, with great gratitude and humility, I learned to accept and honor what other people saw in me. This truly became my "emotional fuel for life," which inspired further growth and development. In reality, when we acknowledge these "gems" in ourselves and in others, we are praising God, who has endowed us with these gifts. In that sense, who are we not to acknowledge and honor them?

> Our deepest fear is not that we are inadequate. Our deepest fear is that we are powerful beyond measure. It is our light, not our darkness that most frightens us. We ask ourselves, "Who am I to be brilliant, gorgeous, talented, fabulous?" Actually, who are you not to be? You are a child of God. Your playing small does not serve the world. There is nothing enlightened about shrinking so that other people won't feel insecure around you. We are all meant to shine, as children do. We were born to make manifest the glory of God that is within us. It's not just in some of us; it's in everyone. And as we let our own light shine, we unconsciously give other people permission to do the same. As we are liberated from our own fear, our presence automatically liberates others. (Williamson, *A Return to Love*, 190-91)

When it came to the third step, that of "rejecting strokes" that did not feel authentic or growth promoting, I had to struggle mightily to let go of these. Like many of us who are super critical of ourselves, I heartily agreed with any veiled or crooked criticism that came my way: "They have discovered who you really are!" Over time, I have learned to take the source of these comments into account and not waste time analyzing or getting despondent over them. Additionally, if I am motivated from an empowered position, I can look objectively at the veiled criticism disguised as a stroke, and decipher any valid information that might be useful for my own spiritual transformation.

Asking for strokes involves overcoming a lot of inner resistance and a lot of practice. But practice I did, and I gradually learned to acknowledge the empowering practicality of this step. Of course, we should not ignorantly expose ourselves to people we don't trust; it is best to practice this activity within our most intimate relationships. If I ask my spouse for a stroke and he says "No," it is good to remember that "no" does not mean "never"; it may be that the timing was just not right. I have to learn to appreciate my effort in asking for a stroke, almost regardless of the outcome. I learned that this kind of conscious vulnerability, far from being weakness, was a sign of an authentic, empowered self. As with any new behavior, it took practice, practice, practice! Once again, it is helpful to return to 'Abdu'l-Bahá's counsel: "Little by little, day by day."

Putting into practice the fifth step of "stroking the self" was the most challenging. As we go down the list of the five items meant to enhance one's "stroke economy," they become progressively more difficult to do. As I went down the list, the external cultural and religious taboos grew stronger. Internally, there was a mighty battle between my overdeveloped "Critical Parent," seemingly backed by God, and my fledgling, emergent authentic self, attempting to shed light on and question some of the absolute attributions and assumptions made about my character. This struggle was, as I mention in Part I, an inner spiritual court martial. In overcoming this battle, which can still flare up from time to time (but never as one-sidedly brutal as it did in the initial phases), the involvement of my objective "Adult," my "Nurturing Parent," feedback from other trusted friends, and above all else, guidance from the Writings and other sane informative writers, were indispensable tools and allies.

To the extent that I have put all the five steps of the stroke economy into practice, my life and the life of those around me—family, friends, and group members—have become greatly enriched and authentic. I believe that the quality of life in any community, whether it is work, church, the Bahá'í community, or any other gathering, could be enhanced by applying these steps to translating "that which has been written into reality and action" Bahá'u'lláh, *Gleanings*, 250).

I have experienced many Bahá'í communities at various levels of stroke deprivation, wherein the gatherings become formal, dry, and often boring. This passage from the Guardian was revealing and confirming of this notion:

> ...*the believers have not yet fully drawn on each other's love for strength and consolation in time of need. The Cause of God is endowed with tremendous powers, and the reason the believers do not gain more from it is because they have not learned to duly draw on these mighty forces of love and strength and harmony generated by the faith.* (Shoghi Effendi, "Living the Life," 9)

See also these passages by 'Abdu'l-Bahá, which point to a level of intimate, authentic and loving relationship:

> *Concern yourselves with one another. Help along one another's projects and plans. Grieve over one another. Let none in the whole country go in need. Befriend one another until ye become as a single body, one and all.*
>
> ('Abdu'l-Bahá, in Universal House of Justice, *Compilation of Compilations*, Vol. 1, 98–99)

> *Order your lives in accordance with the first principle of the divine teaching, which is love.*
>
> ('Abdu'l-Bahá, *Promulgation of Universal Peace*, 8)

Of course, we should keep in mind that all of these efforts we make, through the guidance of the Writings and using these therapeutic tools, are gradual and often painstaking steps toward our goal of spiritual transformation. We should also be aware that our supreme and ultimate goal is to be accepted and praised by God:

> *If one is praised and chosen by God, the accusations of all the creatures will cause no loss to him; and if the man is not accepted in the Threshold of God, the praise and admiration of all men will be of no use to him.* ('Abdu'l-Bahá, *Tablets of 'Abdu'l-Bahá Abbás*, 158)

This ultimate goal is perhaps unattainable by most of us. If I think of 'Abdu'l-Bahá's description of a tree's process of gradual growth, to me the above passage would represent the tree in its fullest maturation. It does not benefit us or others to pretend that we have reached this state of complete renunciation, when we simply have not!

Part IV
Putting Everything into Practice

The Role of Tests and Difficulties on the Journey Toward Wholeness and Authenticity

> The authentic self is the soul made visible.
> —Sarah B. Breathnach (*Simple Abundance*, Foreword)

"I swear by my life! Nothing save that which profiteth them can befall my loved ones. To this testifieth the Pen of God, the Most Powerful, the All-Glorious, the Best Beloved" (Bahá'u'lláh, as quoted in Shoghi Effendi, *Advent of Divine Justice*, 82). Really?! This utterance, like many others from Bahá'u'lláh, can be confounding if we perceive it merely with our human understanding, or if we take it at the level of our physical or material reality. We can cite many examples from our own life, or the lives of some wonderful people we know, who seem to be confronted with a continuous series of seemingly insurmountable challenges or tragedies. These examples appear to belie Bahá'u'lláh's statement by raising the following question: "How could so many bad things happen to good people?" There may be an additional introspective inquiry as well: "Am I suffering these calamities because I am not one of His loved ones?" A part of us connotes catastrophic events—the loss of a loved one, financial ruin, or other challenges that threaten our health or wellbeing—with punishment, and therefore not being seen or loved by God. Some predictable reactions may be confusion, feeling victimized, depression, or anger toward the particular event(s), or even God. In fact, many people at this juncture part ways with their belief or trust in God, asking, "If there is a God, why would He let this happen to me or mine?" Or you might hear statements such as this: "I prayed so hard for a particular outcome and my prayers did not work; therefore, I no longer believe in God!"

So, this passage from Bahá'u'lláh only makes sense if we combine it with the rest of the guidance and precepts that have been bestowed upon us, according to my limited understanding and lived experience. This view of reality requires me to fully comprehend and accept myself as, first and foremost, a spiritual being in a physical body that lasts for up to a hundred years, which is less than the blink of an eye compared the eternity for which I am told my soul will continue to exist and grow. The main purpose of my temporal existence is to nurture and develop my spiritual side, even as I attend to my physical and material wellbeing. This "Owner's Manual" says that I should never lose sight of the primary reason for my creation, which is "to know and to worship God." He has tied this purpose inextricably to the act of me getting to know my true self—my spiritual side, in which my Creator has deposited some of His own names and attributes, such as beauty, mercy, justice, and the like. All of life's incidents and accidents, be they glorious or catastrophic, ought to be subservient to this main purpose; excessive attachment to anything or anybody can divert my attention and focus away from this purpose.

As I follow this prescription, there is a total paradigm shift, in light of which the above passage makes perfect sense. His "loved ones" become those who have committed themselves to the pursuit of understanding the "Owner's Manual." In that light, the external events of my life simply (not to be confused with *easily*) become lessons, corrections, and adjustments, which He promises will be for my spiritual growth and benefit. If I have my eyes on the ultimate prize of getting continuously closer to who my Creator says I can be, I am not only not exempt from tests and difficulties, I expect and accept them. Maybe one day, I will even welcome them as vital elements of my soul's journey toward God.

One of the greatest honors of my life—spiritually, personally, and professionally—were the three trips to Haifa with Jack in 1996, 1997, and 1998 to present workshops on communication skills. Here, once again, was an example of the mysterious interconnections of our lives and the lives of our beloved friends, the MacQueens, who were invited to serve in Haifa in 1995. Julian, having experienced our work in his Innisfree Hotels organization, recommended that the House of Justice ask us to conduct these workshops for a few of the volunteer staff departments in Haifa. Each trip was of two to three weeks duration, and they were the ultimate honor and joyful highlight of our combined careers. Jack and I felt that all that we had learned and experienced up to that point, both professionally and in terms of Bahá'í service, had been in preparation for these trips. We both were in utter disbelief, filled with awe and deep gratitude that we had the opportunity to do the work we loved and felt passionate about on the mountain of God! It was also nerve wracking, at least for me—I have never prayed as hard for guidance from Bahá'u'lláh.

Another event that radically changed the course of my life was the diagnosis of Chronic Fatigue Syndrome. Initially, this diagnosis seemed nothing short of a calamitous event, and its timing made it all the more shocking and mysterious to me. Prior to my diagnosis, while I was in New York in 1995 for work as a multicultural consultant, I had the bounty and pleasure of attending a fund-raising event for the completion of the Ark, at which Mr. Alí Nakhjavání was representing the House of Justice. Given that Mr. Nakhjavání had been one of my heroes, I could not believe my luck for this well-timed coincidence.

There were several hundred friends at this gathering. There was one sentence in his talk that jumped out at me, which seemed to say "that we should beg Bahá'u'lláh to interfere in our lives." My automatic and silly thought was he probably meant "intervene." Then, as if he had miraculously read my mind, he added, "Friends, and I mean *interfere*." He elaborated on what "interfere" meant by saying, "You have prayed with all your heart and mind around a particular issue. You have decided to go North, then you pray to Bahá'u'lláh to interfere in your life and He turns you around and says 'You are going South!'" Well, I could not get this out of my mind. In 1997, when Jack and I had the bounty of going on Pilgrimage, every time we went to the Holy Shrines, I begged Bahá'u'lláh to interfere in my life—and about two or three weeks after we came back, I got sick.

The first stage of the illness was of utter confusion, staying in bed for four or five days, and being just as exhausted as the first day I was bedridden. The usual questions of "Why me? Why now?" presented themselves. I reminded myself of a phrase by 'Abdu'l-Bahá that says, "God will answer the prayer of every servant if that prayer is urgent" (*Promulgation of Universal Peace*, 246). I definitely prayed with urgency, begging Bahá'u'lláh to interfere in my life! Was this how He was interfering in my life? Is there a lesson here for me, and if so, what is it? I once again prayed to God to help me in my confusion.

While looking up Writings for an upcoming Feast (the Bahá'í monthly community gathering), I came upon this passage, which leapt off the page at me:

> *I beseech God to ordain prosperity unto thee in this world, to confer favor upon thee in His supreme Kingdom, and to heal thee from the illness which has befallen thee for some hidden reason which no one knows save God. Verily the Will of God engages occasionally in some matter for which mankind is unable to find out the reason. The causes and reasons shall appear. Trust in*

God and confide in Him, and resign thyself to the Will of God. Verily, thy God is affectionate, compassionate and merciful. He will look at thee with the glances of the eye of mercifulness, will guard thee with the eye of bounty, and will cause His mercy to descend upon thee. ('Abdu'l-Bahá, *The Divine Art of Living*, 59)

It is said that a "miracle is in the eye of the beholder." For one thing, subsequent editions of the book did not include this passage that spoke to me so personally; however, it is attributed to 'Abdu'l-Bahá in Vol. 8 of *Star of the West*, an early 20th-century Bahá'í magazine. For another, the act of reading it was as real as 'Abdu'l-Bahá reaching down to me and saying:

1. You are not abandoned or forgotten by God.
2. It is OK for you to be confused; only God knows the reason.
3. If you stay vigilant, conscious, and prayerful, you will know the reason.
4. Be accepting and resigned to what is.
5. Your God is affectionate — in my state of utter helplessness, the adjective "affectionate" felt powerfully personal, meaningful, and intimate.

After reading this passage, I felt truly seen, heard, and loved by God. It brought much solace to my confused mind and soul.

After the initial CFS diagnosis in 1997, I continued with my practice and my Bahá'í service for two more years, periodically hitting the proverbial wall, staying in bed for a few days, and then soldiering on. In 1999, I became really ill: I was bedridden for several weeks, closed my practice, cancelled all workshops and activities, resigned from the Local Spiritual Assembly (an administrative body that serves a local Bahá'í community), and had to go on disability! By the standards of the world, I was reduced to nothing. At first it was terrifying, devastating, and depressing; to be stripped of my various identities left me naked, helpless, and at a total loss. Invariably I would ask myself, "Who am I now?"

When you are flat on your back and unable to do anything else, you have lots and lots of time to think! Every personal issue I ever had — or didn't know I had — came to the forefront. Ultimately, what saved me was putting (or attempting to put) my spiritual truths and the practical tools of psychotherapy into practice…step by painful step. As one of Jack Guillebeaux's favorite phrases describes, "This is where the rubber hits the road." I had ample time to consider how a certain passage from the Writings or a tool from therapy might apply to my situation.

One of the passages from *The Hidden Words* of Bahá'u'lláh that I have learned to turn to whenever I am undergoing a test reads as follows: "My calamity is my providence, outwardly it is fire and vengeance, but inwardly it is light and mercy" (15). "Providence," which I looked up, refers to "the care, guardianship, and control exercised by a deity, divine direction." Here, my belief is put to the test: if I believe that the author of these words is my Creator, given all that I know about Him—I know that He created me out of love, He knows me better than I will ever be able to know myself, and the goal of His overarching guidance is nothing but my wellbeing in this life and the next—then I owe it to Him and to myself to confidently and patiently look for the promised, if perhaps at the moment too well-hidden, "light and mercy." This, of course, was extremely challenging when I was in the "calamity, fire and vengeance" phase! Here again we have the gift (or the curse) of freedom of choice; we can choose to remain in the "calamity" ("Why me? Why now?") phase, or choose to have faith and conscious knowledge, and actively look for the gifts of "providence." In my own experience, I have realized that the ability to recognize the gifts often requires spiritual growth on my part. Since He wants me to be "golden," I have to sacrifice my "copper-hood," and let go of parts of myself. This is never easy! Bahá'u'lláh alludes to this process of transformation in *Prayers and Meditations*:

> *I beg of Thee, O my God, by Thy most exalted Word which Thou hast ordained as the Divine Elixir unto all who are in Thy realm, the Elixir through whose potency the crude metal of human life hath been transmuted into purest gold…* (54)

Here, I go from the sublime to the ridiculous by sharing an anecdote with the same spiritual truth and message at a very base, all-too-human level. As the story goes, a very wealthy man died, and in his will he gave his eldest son all his material possessions; to the middle son, he left all his productive lands; and to the youngest son, he bequeathed a barn full of manure! Those who knew of this were deeply concerned for the youngest son and went looking for him, expecting to find him in despair. Instead, they found him joyfully singing as he shoveled the manure in the barn. Astonished at this scene and thinking that he had gone mad, they asked him how he could be so upbeat. He responded by saying, "Any time there is this much manure, there ought to be a pony somewhere!" I relate this crude analogy to a spiritual verity by considering that when we are in the "fire, vengeance" phase, it may feel just as improbable or impossible to see any good in the situation—and that is exactly when we have to act out of faith, despite our baser and extremely human impulses.

I am now in the 23rd year of living with CFS, and although strides have been made toward at least accepting and legitimizing this condition as an illness—albeit a mysterious one, since its etiology is still unknown despite abounding theories—there is as yet no cure, although at least there are some treatments. Its more recent acceptance as a "bona fide illness" means that at least sufferers are no longer told, "It's all in your head; there is nothing wrong with you!"

The psychosomatic explanation is exactly what some of the early sufferers heard in the 1950s—mostly women, at least at that time. The documentary film *I Remember Me,* made by Kim Snyder in 2001, included interviews with a group of women who described their initial horrifying experiences when they came down with the mysterious "flu." In the film, a group of these women—now in their 70s and 80s—reunited on camera. While they celebrated together the newer attitudes toward their mysterious illness, what was perhaps more important was that they felt vindicated at last, in their later years. Their long-awaited vindication was largely due to the hubris on the part of the mid-century medical professionals who seemed to say, "What you are describing as your experience does not exist in my medical books, therefore it is not real; hence, you must be crazy." In addition to the element of hubris, there was also a heavy dose of sexism at work; women were considered too emotional, and not taken seriously. Even in the 1980s and 1990s, CFS was referred to as the "yuppie flu," implying that the sufferers (at that time still mostly women) were bored suburban professionals who somehow developed imaginary symptoms. I had a firsthand experience with this attitude: once, I asked a physician acquaintance if he had seen any cases of CFS in his practice. His response was, "No, we live in a semi-rural area and deal only with real illnesses!" As the years have gone by, evidence has shown that there are actually many male sufferers as well, a fact that perhaps has helped legitimize this condition.

So, when I prayed and begged Bahá'u'lláh to "interfere" in my life, I came down with this devastating, life altering, and mysterious illness! It could be argued that the two had nothing to do with each other, and the timing was simple coincidence; what matters is that for me there was a direct correlation. In another sense, however, the cause and effect of it really doesn't matter. What was indisputable was that it was a Major Test! Jack, referring to the potential correlation between my prayer and the outcome, would semi-teasingly say, "Fafar, please leave me out of your prayers."

When it came time to harvest the gifts of this cataclysmic earthquake in my life, I was forced to go to the deepest levels of my inner being. Like all spiritual tests, there were severe challenges to some of my fundamental assumptions, which until then composed the only inner map I had. Once again, I was confronted by the fact that what I considered solid ground had been nothing but quicksand! Each test, I believe, provides us an opportunity to remove a layer of "vain imagining" or illusion to get us closer to spiritual truth, which is the only reality. As a saying goes, "Whatever has been the problem, if it brings you to prayer, it has already served its purpose!"

I suppose at its most fundamental level, the gift of curtailment of my outer activities was the magnificent opportunity to focus on my inner life and being. On a visit to the beach, I wrote this passage, which spoke of my puzzling experience at the time:

"On Being…"

> I think, at least lately, I am more a "be-er" than a "do-er"! As soon as I say this, I can hear objections and protests from friends and family, reminding me of the busy schedule I keep. In my mind I see their smiling faces barely tolerating my self-assessment. I can observe a range of reactions from amazed disbelief to impatient frustration as they each give me a version of "but you're constantly on the go!" Maybe my claiming the status of "be-er" is a delayed reaction to all the periods of busy "doings" in my life. All I know is that I now have an organismic rebellion towards "frenzied doing."
>
> Maybe I distrust and dislike the assumption that what we're doing is so important that we cannot slow down, our own sense of indispensability?!
>
> Maybe we drown ourselves in activity in order to drown out the Loud Whisperings of our soul!
>
> Maybe puppet-like we yield into unconscious activity as the ancestors still pull the strings.
>
> Maybe fueled by the fear of finding no-thing within, we grasp at any and all of other people's agendas.
>
> Maybe the fear is far from finding no-thing within.
>
> Maybe the fear is of finding something so objectionable, we could not fathom facing!
>
> Maybe we have never quite accepted the gift of our "Being" and in our

quiet or clamorous desperation decided "to do" in order to earn the right "to be"?

Maybe we parted ways with our "Being" so long ago we fear "Not Being" if we're not doing?

"I Do, therefore I Am?"

Farzaneh, September 1998

With hindsight, I can see that I was, largely unconsciously, revisiting and updating my answers to the three basic questions:

1. Who am I?
2. Who are the others?
3. How will I make it?

Having been brought to my knees or fallen flat on my face, I was forced to acknowledge the limitations and the inaccuracies of my former answers.

If we think of the "Okay Corral" and the three quadrants that represent the various potential cells of the "prison of self" in light of the fact that our Creator wants us to constantly, continuously move toward the reality of the fourth quadrant, tests and difficulties can be viewed as opportunities for us to identify the particular bar(s), albeit imaginary, of our unique quadrant and use our "knowledge, volition, and action" ('Abdu'l-Bahá, *Foundations*, 101) to bring us closer to the "I+ U+" Quadrant.

One of the most fundamental elements of my self-definition was the notion that "I am not enough." As explained in an earlier chapter (Part II: "Getting to Know Me"), this notion grew from the extremely high expectations of my parents and my own interpretations of those mandates. Since their expectations were based on and aligned with the Writings, and since I was highly motivated to please them and make them proud, I felt obligated to excel in everything. Perfection seemed to be the goal. Mistakes, which represented weakness and failure, were to be avoided like the plague. Of course, it was not the intention of my beloved parents to put me in this spiritual perfectionistic straitjacket, but when assisted by some of my own innate qualities and characteristics, that became its effect.

Given that perfection is an impossible goal, the impact of me pursuing and (of course) coming face to face with my inadequacies brought me to the conclusion that I was not enough or good enough; there was something fundamentally and irrevocably wrong with me! Therefore, in 1999, confronted by a forced retirement from all aspects of my life, it seemed like the Universe (God) was saying, "So you thought you were not doing enough and were not good enough? Let's see how you're going to handle not being able to do anything and unable to please anybody!"

Fruits of CFS

> We must be willing to get rid of the life we've planned,
> so as to have the life that is waiting for us.
> —Joseph Campbell (*Reflections*, 18)

It is said that there are three *correncias* in any intimate relationship: (1) time, (2) energy, and (3) strokes (defined here as a primary unit of recognition; giving praise and appreciation to the other), and we can evaluate a relationship by how well we attend to these currencies. There is an abundance of each of these elements, and we are in charge of how we use them. We all have the same amount of time, 24 hours a day—energy is renewable and strokes are often abundantly returned to us.

CFS, which turned my life upside down and forced me to abandon most outward activities, also provided me the opportunity to focus on my inner life. I knew that Bahá'u'lláh wants us to have a loving and intimate relationship with Him. Applying the three currencies to what should be my most intimate relationship with my Creator and His most Supreme Manifestation, Bahá'u'lláh, I was granted a lot of time to ponder and focus on the quality of my relationship to Him. When it came to "energy," the second currency, it was often a challenge. However, with complete bed rest—sometimes for a day or many days in a row—I was fortunately able to regain some level of energy. The third currency, "strokes," urges me to examine the quality of my relationship, with its emphasis on active participation to create a loving, intimate connection. Here, one of the "Hidden Words" was particularly helpful.

"O SON OF BEING! Love Me, that I may love thee. If thou lovest Me not, My love can in no wise reach thee. Know this O servant" (Bahá'u'lláh, *Hidden Words*, 4). These words made me realize that my active participation is crucial in creating this loving bond. How incredibly, divinely empowering is that? This thought forced me to examine some of the conditions I had put on this most important relationship: would Bahá'u'lláh love me now that I couldn't do much outwardly? This question also required that I enter this divine experiment with an open heart and mind. Would He grace me with His love in my current condition of inactivity? During this ongoing and very personal experiment, I would sometimes beg Bahá'u'lláh to show me a sign that could help me understand that He saw, heard, and loved me. Invariably, the answers would come in many different forms. Sometimes it would be just a deep feeling of loving peacefulness, a sense that "all is well." At other times, it could be a kind, impactful card, or a call from a friend or a former client.

Another passage felt like nothing but pure, unconditional love: "The whole duty of man in this day is to attain that share of the flood of grace which God poureth forth for him" (Bahá'u'lláh, *Gleanings*, 8). Wow — "flood of grace" spoke to me of an ultimate abundance of unconditional love, and it is my "duty" to attain and receive it. This passage deeply comforted my soul, and made me think that maybe I would be okay!

Yet another passage that was deeply comforting was by Shoghi Effendi, our beloved Guardian:

> *The troubles of this world pass and what we have left is what we have made of our souls, so it is to this we must look — to becoming more spiritual, drawing nearer to God, no matter what our human minds and bodies go through.* (*Directives from the Guardian*, 68)

From these words I deduced two good-news, bad-news conclusions. The bad news? "Yes, you have been given a mysterious, often confounding chronic condition." The good news, though, was as follows: "You could use this as an opportunity to attend to your soul and spiritual side, which is the more important part of the agenda." This realization was a lucid and comforting clarification of priorities.

Here, I must acknowledge another one of God's blessings in the person of my beloved physician, Dr. Teresa Allen. Given that in 1997 there were very few doctors who recognized CFS as a disease or knew what (or how) to do anything about it, her presence in Montgomery was nothing short of a miracle. She began her career journey as a nurse; later, she earned her medical degree in osteopathy. After practicing in the mainstream medical model for about five years, she became aware of its serious limitations. She then transitioned into an integrative, alternative practitioner at great financial sacrifice, fighting an ongoing and uphill battle. Her innate curiosity, humility, compassion and, above all, her reliance on God and her cellular level commitment to do His will made her an absolute angel of mercy to me and to numerous others who had the bounty of being her patients.

I believe we both felt a soul connection at my very first appointment, which coincidentally fell on Valentine's Day, 1998. Due to her authentically spiritual nature, brilliant mind, humility, and loving patience, any encounter with her was truly healing. Our relationship soon became one of mutual respect, profound spiritual connection, and abiding love. I truly cannot fathom, nor do I want to, going through the CFS journey without her. Thank you, my beloved physician and friend of my heart and soul! To me, she is a living example of this passage by 'Abdu'l-Bahá:

> *O thou distinguished physician!...Praise be to God that thou hast two powers: one to undertake physical healing and the other spiritual healing. Matters related to man's spirit have a great effect on his bodily condition. For instance, thou shouldest impart gladness to thy patient, give him comfort and joy, and bring him to ecstasy and exultation. How often hath it occurred that this hath caused early recovery. Therefore, treat thou the sick with both powers...* (Selections, 150)

CFS also had a profound effect on the direction of my practice. By 1999, even though I was not anywhere close to admitting it to myself, I had become somewhat bored with my practice. So, even though at the time I had to close my practice—which meant letting go of my office—amid much sadness, confusion, and reluctance, in retrospect I comprehend the Divine Wisdom and guidance behind what some might call a failure.

As I look back, I realize that the reason for the diminished joy and excitement in my work was that many of my clients were interested in short-term solutions, not in a comprehensive process of transformation. Of course, there is nothing wrong with seeking short-term solutions and I was quite up to the task of delivering them; however, my soul's yearning was really in the deep-digging, life-long process of spiritual transformation. It would not, of course, have been fair or appropriate for me to lay, even unconsciously, my wishes or expectations for deep transformative work on my clients.

One session that elucidates this dilemma stands out in my mind. In my desire to help raise the consciousness of a particular client beyond a focus on the immediate and often material issues of daily life, I shared the metaphor of the closet versus the refrigerator. This is how it goes: a person who had never seen a refrigerator came upon an abandoned one. He was overjoyed by his discovery of this treasure; he loved and admired its smooth surface, opened its door, examined the various compartments, and was thrilled to have found this most extraordinary *closet*. He imagined what articles of clothing he would put in each compartment! Brimming with pride and joy, he brought a friend to see his found treasure. The friend, who was quite familiar with refrigerators, enlightened his buddy by saying, "You have totally missed the point if you think this is a closet!" Then, he proceeded to plug in the refrigerator and elaborate on its purpose and function.

The moral of the metaphor was that as human beings, we can live our lives entirely at the material level of "closet-hood" — or plug ourselves in to a Higher Power and elevated consciousness by becoming aware of our true function and destiny. What followed was that my client looked at me with all sincerity and seriousness and said, "Fafar, I am happy as a closet and I want to continue being one." Then, we both burst into laughter. This encounter had a significant impact on me; it showed that people are where they are by choice, and in fact it is our God-given freedom of choice in terms of how we want to live our lives. Looking back, I realize that I had outlived my desire to do therapy that was not integrative and deeply transformative. So, as I see it, the Divine hand put an end to that phase of my practice!

Having said that, I continued to lead my two monthly therapy groups at home, attracting Bahá'í and non-Bahá'í participants who were committed to their own journey of transformation. Freed from the strictures of an office practice and blessed with clients who were committed to going beyond "closet-hood," I was able to focus my energies on what had always been my primary goal and motivator: "spiritual transformation." I was delighted to be working with clients who prioritized their spiritual side, and I was freer to share the peaks and valleys of my own journey toward wholeness, an aspect that the participants repeatedly attested was highly significant for them.

There was also a shift in the group membership that was not designed or enforced by me. From the beginning, my groups had both male and female members, but over time those groups became solely women. The wisdom of this evolution dawned on me and the participants. I fully believe that as women we benefit greatly from having a safe, women-centric space as we examine various aspects of our being and doing.

My shift of emphasis from problem-focused short-term therapy (which has a necessary and legitimate place) to deep transformative work resonated with many of the women, who have been group members for years and sometimes affectionately call themselves "lifers." From time to time, an observer or a family member may have made comments to them, such as "Are you still in that group, aren't you well yet?" At some level, that may sound like a legitimate question and observation; throughout the years, especially in the earlier phase of my home-based practice, my own Critical Parent would say something like "Some kind of therapist you are, no one seems to get well and you see some of the same people over and over again!" The passage of time and amazing, insightful, and supportive feedback from participants allows me to now view my shift as a paradigm shift. If we consider this earthly life as a school for us to acquire knowledge about ourselves, our Creator, and the purpose of life—and as an opportunity to bring our life more and more into alignment with the latest overarching guidance from God—then a form of therapy focused on those goals could be, or perhaps needs to be, long-term. In this light, if the therapeutic aim is not just exclusively to eliminate problems but to learn how to perceive those problems as springboards toward that life-long goal of alignment, then the project is never ending. As long as the participants experience and report progress on their unique journey toward wholeness, I am honored and privileged to share my journey with them; I view the whole process as a sacred experiment. In the Bahá'í Writings there are often comparisons between the world of nature and spiritual realities and processes; for example, the Writings describe God as a gardener who tends to each plant according to its particular nature and needs ('Abdu'l-Bahá, *Selections*, 129). Sometimes I have used this imagery myself, seeing the long-term members of my various groups as plants and flowers who have chosen and blessed me by being in my "hothouse." As long as they are growing and blossoming, I am honored to serve them as a gardener who is growing and developing by their side. For me, it doesn't get any better than that!

As I was writing about this metaphor of plants and gardening, I came across these two poems written by a former group member over two decades ago. I was happy to see these verses and felt some reluctance and reservation in using them, lest they be seen as self-aggrandizement. Then, I reconsidered: she wrote about the process which I own, honor, and cherish. I decided to include them here.

> "Transformation in Montgomery"
>
> The Gardener of my soul
> Plowing rows through the
> misconceptions in my mind
> planting seeds of wisdom
> in the barren soil
> watering the sprouts of hope
> with love
> Fertilizing with hugs,
> Feedback and guidance

Removing weeds of self-doubt
grandiosity and doom
cultivating roses of
self-esteem
of love
of joy

— Rachel '96

"Flowers"

Farzaneh is the
gardener of my soul
and the ones growing
with me all
these years
are
mirrors where I
can see myself
if I am not blind and
Teachers from whom I
can learn if
I am willing
some have perfume
some have thorns
all are flowers and
all are beautiful
to my eyes
Thank you
my mirrors and
teachers and
Thank you, Farzaneh,
my gardener, my mentor
and friend of my heart.

— Rachel '97

There were other fruits or bestowed gifts that grew from the outer inactivity and isolation enforced by CFS. Although these gifts may be of lesser significance, they helped to organically create, complete, and give new dimension to this phase of my life.

One such gift: I had always been interested in decorating our home, but I had never had the leisure to focus on what was truly pleasing to my soul. My heightened need and desire for order, beauty, and balance seemed to run a parallel course with my inner struggles with the process of spiritual transformation. In fact, the two paths seemed to greatly affect each other, underlining the interconnectedness of physical and spiritual realities. Growing flowers and arranging them became a creative, highly soul-satisfying activity. Appreciation from family and friends helped galvanize this pursuit.

Fewer activities in the outer world also allowed me to have frequent visits to Athens, Georgia, where our daughter Minou and her lovely family had settled. Being there for the birth of our grandson and our many subsequent visits in the early years of his life were truly sweet blessings.

During this period, I frequently attempted to make my life a personal experiment to experience first-hand the translation of "that which hath been written into reality and action" (Bahá'u'lláh, *Gleanings*, 250). One of these experiments was to compare and contrast the quality of days when I consciously beseeched God for guidance and support against the days that I did not. The qualitative difference between these days helped to make real the necessity and the blessing of beseeching God at all times and under all conditions. In this process, I had to learn deeper levels of patience and submission to what was, rather than what I thought should be—and I struggled to make peace with not knowing or understanding much of what was happening. These words written by Rainer Maria Rilke were helpful:

> Be patient toward all that is unsolved in your heart and try to love the questions themselves like locked rooms or books that are written in a foreign tongue....The point is to live everything. Live the questions now. Perhaps you will then gradually, without noticing it, live your way some distant day into the answer. (*Letters to a Young Poet*, 20)

Developing and experiencing the virtue of patience while resisting the urge of sinking into morbid depression was a mighty challenge. It was known in our family that when my mother was in labor with me, my father had gone to get the midwife—but I was born before their arrival. So, from time to time, when I was displaying impatience, my father was fond of saying, "You came to the world in haste and you have been in a hurry ever since." This was said affectionately, and maybe even with some pride.

As always, identifying and lifting things up to the level of spiritual principle was the ultimate paradigm shift:

> O Son of Man! For everything there is a sign. The sign of love is fortitude under My decree and patience under My trials. (Bahá'u'lláh, *Hidden Words*, 15)

Learning to accept and cope with CFS was often in the background during some of my life's most horrendous and potentially soul-shattering tests. I believe that parents would universally attest to the fact that nothing can bring us to our knees with utter helplessness and despair as when our kids are in trouble! I have already alluded to our daughter Minou's experience of cancer in 1995–1996, when she was 24 years old. Praise be to God she came through it—not only cancer free, but with great spiritual insights. When she was diagnosed, I initially went to my predictable place of feeling guilty and making it my fault: either I should have been able to prevent it somehow, or I was being punished through my innocent child for my shortcomings past and present. Either way, I felt remote from God.

However, thanks to the internet and the healing prayers pouring from all parts of the globe, I never felt alone or punished in isolation. The impact of this network of love and support, added to my own urgent and often desperate prayers, was truly magical. For the first time in my life I experienced the reality of feeling God's love, even as everything seemed to be going wrong. To my utter surprise, I began to feel a deep sense of joy and wellness even before the happy outcome. I distinctly remember several times that I felt light and joyful on the inside when friends and family called with sadness and deep concern; I had a new sense that everything would be okay, almost regardless of the outcome. This feeling is illustrated by Dame Julian of Norwich, a 13th-century English mystic— and I have often found comfort in these simple words:

> All shall be well,
> And all shall be well,
> And all manner of things
> shall be well.
> (*Revelations of Divine Love*, 79)

This new sense of profound inner peace and wellness in the middle of scary chaos was the gift of my young daughter's bout with cancer.

Naturally, this period of facing tests and difficulties was not all doom and gloom by any means; there were also gloriously happy events and times. One of these was the marriage of our Minou, who had gone through her own tests and difficulties at a young age, to our beloved Robert Rysiew. Throughout the years my friend Kim and I had expressed a wish that we could be relatives as well as best friends. Since Rob is Kim's nephew, our wish was truly fulfilled. In 1995, when Kim and I took a trip to Canada, I had briefly met Rob at the home of his parents, Bill and Brenda Rysiew. I felt an immediate affinity for this couple, as if I had always known them— one of those mysterious feelings that do not appear to make any sense at the time. I was totally clueless that this lovely couple would be our Minou's in-laws.

At this juncture Rob, their youngest son, was rather at loose ends in his life. Kim and Julian, the kind-hearted aunt and uncle, invited him to come to Pensacola, Florida, offered him a job at one of Julian's hotels, and Kim offered Rob ten therapy sessions with—in her words—"the best therapist I know." That would be moi! During those ten sessions, I got to know and love Rob inside and out. At the last session, as he was leaving my office, he glanced at a picture of Minou on my desk and asked me, "And who is this gorgeous woman?" I replied, "That happens to be my daughter!" I must have shared this with Kim, because then our joint mission became making sure that these two at least met. So, shortly before Rob returned to Canada, they met at Kim and Julian's home, unaware that they would be gloriously joined for life in that same house!

Kim and I, having seen the spark between them, wanted to be encouraging and supportive of its continuation and development. After Rob returned home, they established an email relationship. By this time, Kim and Julian had begun their service in the Holy Land; however, their kindness and generosity were never far away. When Minou had to have surgery and radiation for her Squamous Cell Carcinoma, they bought a ticket for Rob to come to Alabama to be with all of us at that most difficult and scary juncture! His loving presence contributed greatly to Minou's spirits, and I think that was the beginning of their commitment to each other. Over the next four years, they continued and deepened their relationship through emails, and Minou went to live with the senior Rysiews in Vancouver for a few months, just as Rob came to live with us in Montgomery. So, by the year 2000, we all knew and loved each other; all of us were eager to celebrate their union at their wedding in Kim and Julian's house. What a blessed chapter!

A year later, with the arrival of their son, Joshua Ali, I was blessed with experiencing the sweetness of that relationship. Another benefit of the curtailment of my too-busy-life pre-CFS was having the opportunity to spend a lot of quality time with Minou and her precious new family; this period also gave Minou and me a chance to forge a new phase of our adult–adult relationship. This gift was made possible by us going for some gut-wrenching, intense family therapy with our beloved Dr. Jo Lewis. Through the grace of God and Jo's brilliant insight and skills, we were able to heal some long-standing, neglected wounds.

Our son endured his own tribulations as well. To put it succinctly, he came within an inch of losing his life. Praise be to God that he is alive through the power of prayer, the instrumentality of a treatment center, and his own prodigious efforts to turn his life around; he is now living a healthy God-centered life, one day at a time.

Through this therapeutic experience with my daughter, as well as through our son's later ordeals, I came to realize and grasp the reality that we can inadvertently deeply hurt our kids just by our being, as well as by the life circumstances we create and impose on them. In our case, my husband and I had prayerfully and joyfully created an interracial family in the South, one rooted in our commitment to the Faith and our love for each other. We were not ignorant of the challenges our progeny would face as bi-racial children and youth; in fact, in order to offset some of the damage from the outside world, we took them to many Bahá'í events and Schools where they were cherished as being unique and as fulfillments of the Bahá'í principle of racial unity.

At the same time, I feel that we were not fully aware, nor perhaps could we afford to let ourselves be aware, of the deeply troubled waters they had to navigate. Of course, I know that being bi-racial was far from the only challenge they faced. I think they, along with other Bahá'í youth of their generation, experienced the deep chasm between Bahá'í standards of conduct (e.g., strict adherence to the law of chastity, the prohibition of drugs and alcohol) and the permissive and highly materialistic society in which they lived. I believe many young people came away from that chasm either feeling a mixture of guilt and shame for having compromised some of the Bahá'í standards, or experiencing a sense of isolation and "differentness" when they did adhere to the high standards of the Faith.

I also believe that for this generation of Bahá'ís, as it was for our children, the chasm was so wide and their experiences so profoundly challenging that they didn't feel they could share them with us as parents. I think that very few Bahá'í youth of that era came through unscathed, and many left the Faith. My heart goes out to them and their parents: I believe we as Bahá'í parents, and the community at large, were often unable or unwilling to partner with them in their sometimes challenging dilemmas that were greatly at variance with Bahá'í standards of conduct. I should add that many others of that generation weathered the storms and are now joyfully serving the Cause of God as they raise their own children.

At the personal level I recognized, as a result of our family therapy sessions, that the gap between my own upbringing and expectations and what our kids were experiencing was so wide that I literally could not afford or allow myself to recognize some of the clues they were putting in front of our faces. After the initial feeling of deep sadness and guilt for my blindness, I came to accept and make peace, with the help of God and our therapist, with the fact that I had done the best that I was capable of doing at that time. I had to comprehend this in order to be able to ask my kids' forgiveness and, similarly, forgive myself. The following Tribute to the Greatest Holy Leaf is highly illuminating:

> Something greater than forgiveness she had shown in meeting the cruelties and strictures in her own life. To be hurt and to forgive is saintly but far beyond this is the power to comprehend and not be hurt. This power she had. The word mazlúm, which signifies acceptance without complaint, has come to be associated with her name. She was never known to complain or lament. It was not that she made the best of things, but that she found in everything, even in calamity itself, the gems of enduring wisdom....She was never impatient. She was as incapable of impatience as she was of revolt. But this was not so much long-sufferance as it was quiet awareness of the forces that operate in the hours of waiting and inactivity. Always she moved with the larger rhythm, the wider sweep, toward the ultimate goal. Surely, confidently, she followed the circle of her orbit round the Sun of her existence, in that complete acquiescence, that perfect accord, which underlies faith itself. (Marjorie Morten, in *The Bahá'í World Vol. 5*, 185)

Witnessing the challenges that our kids went through, I came away with a much deeper understanding and appreciation for the attribute of detachment and the illusion of control. Until then, my feelings about detachment were that it was cold withdrawal, a letting go. Later, I realized that detachment, if correctly understood and practiced, sets the boundaries of who I am, what I can do, and what is beyond me. Regardless of all my prayers and efforts, I am not in charge of what happens in another person's life—and that is really a good thing! I believe that when we want to control the outcome of any situation, in or out of awareness, we are playing God. We forget that ultimately everything is in God's hands, and *that* reality is also a very good thing.

In the next chapter, we turn to another vital tool for the process of spiritual transformation; namely, the proper use of our God-given ability to feel and express a variety of emotions.

"Being Happy, a Delectable Duty"

> We must have the stubbornness to accept our gladness in the ruthless furnace of this world.
> —Jack Gilbert (in Fassler, "The Stubborn Gladness," par. 17)

> Gloom we have always with us, a rank and sturdy weed, but joy requires tending.
> —commonly attributed to Barbara Holland

As Bahá'ís we are quite familiar with the concept of duty, and these are just a few that come to mind:

- The duty to know and love God
- The duty to share the Message of Bahá'u'lláh and teach, teach, teach
- The duty to contribute to the Fund
- The duty to pray
- The duty to work on our own characters
- The duty to serve on administrative bodies if elected
- The duty to obey the mandates of the Universal House of Justice
- The duty to work in the spirit of service

There are many other "duties," such as responsibly raising our families, paying taxes, and so on. Sometimes, we might feel overwhelmed by the sheer volume of our duties: on top of all of those obligations, we are then mandated to be happy? Yes indeed.

If we are not happy and joyous in this season, for what other season shall we wait and for what other time shall we look?

('Abdu'l-Bahá, in *Bahá'í World Faith*, 35)

Be assured and happy.

('Abdu'l-Bahá, *Tablets of 'Abdu'l-Bahá Abbás*, 119)

The soul of man must be happy no matter where he is. One must attain to that condition of inward beatitude and peace, then outward circumstances will not alter his spiritual calmness and joyousness.

('Abdu'l-Bahá, *Star of the West*, Vol. 8, 172)

I want you to be happy...to laugh, smile and rejoice in order that others may be made happy by you.

('Abdu'l-Bahá, *Promulgation of Universal Peace*, 218)

The duty to be happy sounds like a contradiction in terms, since we often and perhaps unconsciously equate happiness with events that happen to us and make us happy. When compared to very serious duties, such as obeying the Laws or teaching the Cause, the mandate to be happy somehow does not quite feel as lofty. It may feel selfish or unworthy of our attention or focus.

There is this amazing passage about "duty" by Bahá'u'lláh: "The whole duty of man in this day is to attain that share of the flood of grace which God poureth forth for him" (*Gleanings*, 8). To the part of us that might associate duty with being burdened and overwhelmed, the above passage may also feel like a contradiction in terms. It is a total paradigm shift to think of my duty to be ready for and receptive to God's overflowing grace washing over me.

Who wouldn't want to fulfill this kind of duty?

Naturally, it all comes down to our definition of happiness. After all, we live in an age and in a culture where a great majority of people are obsessed with the pursuit of happiness, often defined as fulfillment of our physical and material side, or all that we share with the animal kingdom. For animals, meeting their needs is dictated and confined by their biology; they have instinctual needs, not wants.

Some of the characteristics of "happiness" as defined by our culture include the following:

1. *Acquisition of wealth*. This acquisition is preferably gained overnight with minimal effort, often at great cost to others. See, for instance, the scandals of our financial institutions;

pharmaceutical corporations using people in developing nations as guinea pigs to test their drugs, often with lethal side effects; the trafficking of children and youth to be sold into prostitution, and so forth.

2. *Obsession with health.* The cultural obsession with physical health suggests that everyone is in Olympic training. We were never meant to worship our bodies; we were meant to honor them and keep them healthy as the temporary vehicles for our souls. Our pursuit of prolongation of life in any form and at any cost seems to stem from our denial and fear of death.

3. *Pursuit of physical beauty.* This manifests in the drive to becoming a "diva," with all of its implications of blindly following the dictates of a male-dominated fashion industry that promotes anorexic, waif-like young girls as embodiments of ideal, attainable beauty standards. The pursuit can entail extreme make-overs and, for those who can afford them, continuous surgical procedures to alter the shape and size of almost any body part. The use of higher and higher heels that damage the structure of women's feet and spines, and the gifting of daughters with breast reduction or augmentation for major life accomplishments such as graduation, are both symptoms of an overemphasis on physical appearance and its implied promise of happiness and fulfillment.

4. *More fame.* The allure of being adored by thousands or millions leads to people doing practically anything for 15 minutes of fame or infamy—and nobody seems to care about the difference. The explosion of social media technology (e.g., Facebook, tweets, blogs, etc.) has greatly facilitated the pursuit of those goals.

5. *More sexual gratification.* Today, there is a proliferation of pornography that is made easier to access through technology in the comfort of one's home. This abundance blurs the lines regarding what is considered cheating on your marriage partner, not to mention what it does to one's own mind and soul!

6. *Instant, escapist happiness* through drugs and alcohol, which delivers short-term highs and long-lasting or lethal lows.

7. *An excess of profanity* has become commonplace in movies and on TV. "Defile not the tongue with cursing or execration of anyone" ('Abdu'l-Bahá, *A Traveller's Narrative*, 83).

8. *Gratuitous violence* appears not only in movies and on TV, but in children's video games as well, which seems to promote that the essential nature of man is to be violent and aggressive.

> *In the days of old an instinct for warfare was developed in the struggle with wild animals; this is no longer necessary; nay, rather, co-operation and mutual understanding are seen to produce the greatest welfare of mankind. Enmity is now the result of prejudice only.* ('Abdu'l-Bahá, *'Abdu'l-Bahá in London*, 20)

There is nothing wrong with pursuit of most of the above within moderation; as I've mentioned before, God wants us to enjoy this life. The danger lies in the excesses, which are based on a false assumption that we are primarily physical, when we are in fact primarily spiritual and only in a physical body for a very limited time. We as Bahá'ís, the small minority who have heard and accepted the latest Message from God, are mandated to fight against these excessive pursuits, bearing in mind that we are not immune to the dictates of our culture. In fact, we should be alert to the fact that we are bombarded by these overt and covert messages that urge us to acquire more, bigger, and better things. This programming extends itself to our relationships with other people, promoting an attitude of regarding them as objects in our path and treating them as such, to be used or abused as we see fit.

It may have been easier if we, like others in some former dispensations, were given permission to live ascetic lives by withdrawing from society. The opposite is true for us; we are urged to be intimately involved with the concerns of the societies in which we live. We have not been given the option of sitting on the shore and watching the river go by. As Bahá'u'lláh writes in *Gleanings*, "Be anxiously concerned with the needs of the age ye live in, and center your deliberations on its exigencies and requirements" (213). We have to be a part of society, partake of its benefits, and often swim against its current.

> *And yet, how often we seem to forget the clear and repeated warning of our beloved Master, who in particular during the concluding years of His Mission on earth, laid stress on the severe mental tests that would inevitably sweep over His loved ones of the West...tests that would purge, purify and prepare them for their noble mission in life.* (from a letter written by Shoghi Effendi, in Hornby, *Lights of Guidance*, 135)

To the extent that we succeed in viewing our earthly life as described in the Writings, we transform our own being and present the world with an alternative way of being and doing.

So, the prescription for us Bahá'ís is the formidable and magnificent opportunity to bring about a complete paradigm shift by presenting through our own lives, no matter how lowly and humble, a prototype of a new race of man. Characteristic of this new creation is a comprehension, at the cellular level, that we are primarily, fundamentally, undeniably, and unquestioningly spiritual beings put here in this physical form for a very brief but highly purposeful and significant span of time. Understanding this fundamental reality has implications that pervade all aspects of our material and physical life. If, at the core of our being, we have an unshakeable grasp of our spiritual essence, the development of which has been stated as the primary purpose of our physical life, our reactions and responses to life's incidents and accidents will be differently shaped, wisely modified, and greatly moderated.

Bahá'u'lláh says, "Armed with the power of Thy name nothing can ever hurt me, and with Thy love in my heart all the world's afflictions can in no wise alarm me" (*Prayers and Meditations*, 208). What exactly does this statement mean in my life, given that elsewhere He has given us the mandate to "strive to translate that which hath been written into reality and action" (*Gleanings*, 250)? Does it mean that if I am a good Bahá'í, bearing in mind that we are all striving to become good Bahá'ís, I and my loved ones will be protected, shielded from bad or even catastrophic events? Of course not! We know "bad" things happen to "good" people all the time. Does it mean that if I am "armed" with the power of His name, tragedies such as the loss of a loved one, financial calamity, injustice, or natural catastrophes will not impact or hurt me? Once again, the answer is "of course not." I will be devastated, hurt, confused, or driven to ask, "Why is God doing this to me?"

However, if I apply the divine prescription, I will moderate my response by reminding myself of the primary purpose of this life, and witness the miraculous power of that internal paradigm shift. All the world's afflictions may still be there, but I won't be alarmed; I will allow myself to experience the reality that my spiritual core is intact. This reframing, like all other aspects of spiritual growth, is a challenging lifelong process. We should not be dismayed by the inevitable setbacks of this journey.

The following passage further elucidates the absolute necessity of comprehending and allowing ourselves to experience and build upon God's love by magnifying and developing our spiritual reality:

> For every one of you his paramount duty is to choose for himself that on which no other may infringe and none usurp from him. Such a thing – and to this the Almighty is my witness – is the love of God, could ye but perceive it. Build ye for yourselves such houses as the rain and floods can never destroy, which

shall protect you from the changes and chances of this life. (Bahá'u'lláh, *Gleanings*, 261)

Changes and chances are an inevitable part of this physical existence; there is no physical means by which we can shield or protect ourselves from them. Ironically, the only real protection is to develop my inner being, which will allow me to perceive and experience these changes and chances with my inner sight and not be overly confused or alarmed by them. We can progress to a stage that instead of asking, "Why me, God?", we might say, "Thank you God, my faith in you and your love for me is not shaken. Please help me know what minor or major changes I need to make in myself at this point to bring my inner and outer life into alignment with your purpose for my life."

Once again, we are back to the analogy of the "Owner's Manual." If there is an All-Knowing Creator Who brought me into being out of love and Who has placed in me immeasurable potentialities that reflect His own attributes, if He has elaborated that only by developing these potentialities will I truly know myself and yes, become truly "happy," then all my efforts in pursuing and attaining the culturally defined paths to happiness will at best, deliver a limited and passing satisfaction and a feeling of "is that all there is?" Unfortunately, at its worst, this pursuit can lead to catastrophic outcomes for myself and my loved ones.

What is prescribed by the Creator as "happiness" is in line with our fundamental spiritual nature. "The soul of man must be happy no matter where he is. One must attain to that condition of inward beatitude and peace, then outward circumstances will not alter his spiritual calmness and joyousness" ('Abdu'l-Bahá, *Star of the West, Vol. 8*, 172).

In Part IV, "Fruits of CFS," I shared the anecdote about a closet versus a refrigerator, which speaks to the spiritual and physical dual nature of man. This anecdote drives home certain essential points, given the limitations of all analogies:

- We have an outer form, qualities of which we share with the animal kingdom: we eat, sleep, and procreate; we are born and we all die. We have to meet our physical and material needs in order to exist on this earthly plane.

- However, if this is all we do, in all of its manifold shapes and forms, we have missed out on what sets us apart from the animal kingdom (the "closet-hood"), namely our mind and our soul.

- The irony is that we have been given the option of "parking in our 'closet-hood'" to live an unexamined and relatively comfortable life of up to a hundred years.

- Or — "Eureka!" — we can plug ourselves into the Source and realize that although we may *look* like a closet, we are really something totally and marvelously different.

There is another crucial point to be had here: if "it" were only about this physical life, why would we not "park in the closet-hood" where, as Paul Simon says, "[and] we all have a good time!" The big flaw here is that our soul, which our Creator tells us lives eternally, needs to be plugged in to the Source so that with His aid and our own efforts, we can develop potential spiritual qualities and attributes that we will need upon our departure from this limited physical reality. If I find myself spiritually lacking in the next life, the nature of which we are incapable of comprehending through our five senses, I may realize that all the time and energy that I bestowed in this physical realm on perfecting my "closet-hood" to the neglect of my "refrigerator-hood" has left me greatly unprepared, maybe even crippled, for my eternal life. This could be a "I could have had a V-8!" moment.

Another simple analogy: we are like a house that is wired for electricity, but every single time I want light, I am the one who must reach up and flip the switch — or else sit in darkness. I have been given the choice, and there are always consequences to our choices. This passage from the Guardian elucidates this point: "No matter how strong the measure of divine grace, unless supplemented by personal, sustained and intelligent effort, it cannot become fully effective and be of any real and abiding advantage" (Shoghi Effendi, "Living the Life," 7).

What follows is a resource I developed entitled "Being Happy: A Delectable Duty," which can assist in translating spiritual guidance into action. These are practical daily reminders of how to make myself "happy" from the Bahá'í Writings. This is by no means an exhaustive list; it is a humble beginning, and I invite each one to add to it as he/she sees fit.

1. Remind myself that God wants me to be happy.

    a. *O Lord, I have turned my face unto thy Kingdom of Oneness and am drowned in the sea of Thy mercy! O Lord, enlighten my sight by beholding Thy lights in this dark night, and make me happy by the wine of Thy love in this wonderful age!*

        ('Abdu'l-Bahá, *Tablets of 'Abdu'l-Bahá Abbás*, Vol. 3, 676)

    b. *Be assured and happy.*

        ('Abdu'l-Bahá, *Tablets of 'Abdu'l-Bahá Abbás*, Vol. 1, 119)

    c. *Happiness consists of two kinds; physical and spiritual. The physical happiness is limited; its utmost duration is one day, one*

> *month, one year. It hath no result. Spiritual happiness is eternal and unfathomable. This kind of happiness appeareth in one's soul with the love of God and suffereth one to attain to the virtues and perfections of the world of humanity. Therefore, endeavor as much as thou art able in order to illuminate the lamp of thy heart by the light of love.*
>
> ('Abdu'l-Bahá, *Tablets of 'Abdu'l-Bahá Abbás*, Vol. 3, 673)

   d. *The soul of man must be happy no matter where he is. One must attain to that condition of inward beatitude and peace, then outward circumstances will not alter his spiritual calmness and joyousness.*

   ('Abdu'l-Bahá, *Star of the West*, Vol. 8, 172)

   e. *The most great, peerless gift of God to the world of humanity is happiness born of love…*

   ('Abdu'l-Bahá, *Star of the West*, Vol. 13, 103)

2. Say the Greatest Name.

   a. *The Greatest Name should be found upon the lips in the first awakening moment of early dawn. It should be fed upon by constant use in daily invocation, in trouble, under opposition, and should be the last word breathed when the head rests upon the pillow at night. It is the name of comfort, protection, happiness, illumination, love and unity.*

   ('Abdu'l-Bahá, in Hornby, *Lights of Guidance*, 266)

   b. *That the Most Great name exerciseth influence over both physical and spiritual matters is sure and certain.*

   ('Abdu'l-Bahá, from a tablet translated from the Persian titled "Health, Healing and Nutrition," as cited in Universal House of Justice, *Compilation of Compilations*, Vol. 1, 459–88)

3. Pray with joy, certitude, and when I can, with urgency.

   a. *God will answer the prayer of every servant if that prayer is urgent. His mercy is vast, illimitable. He answers the prayers of all His servants. He answers the prayer of this plant. The plant prays potentially, "O God! Send me rain!" God answers the prayer, and the plant grows. God will answer anyone.*

   ('Abdu'l-Bahá, *Promulgation of Universal Peace*, 246)

b. *…only in the remembrance of God can the heart find rest.*

('Abdu'l-Bahá, *Selections*, 96)

c. *Beg everything thou desirest from Bahá'u'lláh. If thou art asking for faith, ask of him. If thou art yearning after knowledge, he will grant it unto thee. If thou art longing for the love of God, he will bestow it upon thee. He will descend upon thee all His blessings.*

('Abdu'l-Bahá, *Star of the West*, Vol. 9, 104)

4. Read the Writings with joy, gratitude, and curiosity.

    Read ye the sacred verses in such measure that ye be not overcome by languor and despondency. Lay not upon your souls that which will weary them and weigh them down, but rather what will lighten and uplift them, so that they may soar on the wings of the Divine verses towards the Dawning-place of His manifest signs; this will draw you nearer to God, did ye but comprehend.

    (Bahá'u'lláh, *The Kitáb-i-Aqdas*, 73)

5. Make knowing and loving myself a priority.

    a. *True loss is for him whose days have been spent in utter ignorance of his self.*

    (Bahá'u'lláh, *Tablets of Bahá'u'lláh*, 156)

    b. *O My servants! Could ye apprehend with what wonders of My munificence and bounty I have willed to entrust your souls, ye would, of a truth, rid yourselves of attachment to all created things, and would gain a true knowledge of your own selves – a knowledge which is the same as the comprehension of Mine Own Being. Ye would find yourselves independent of all else but Me, and would perceive, with your inner and outer eye, and as manifest as the revelation of My Effulgent Name, the seas of My loving-kindness and bounty moving within you.*

    (Bahá'u'lláh, *Gleanings*, 326–27)

    c. *Whatever duty Thou hast prescribed unto Thy servants of extolling to the utmost Thy majesty and glory is but a token of Thy grace unto them, that they may be enabled to ascend unto the station conferred upon their own inmost being, the station of the knowledge of their own selves.*

    (Bahá'u'lláh, *Gleanings*, 4)

d. *The Purpose of the one true God, exalted be His glory, in revealing Himself unto men is to lay bare those gems that lie hidden within the mine of their true and inmost selves.*

(Bahá'u'lláh, *Gleanings*, 287)

6. Take steps to acquire a taste for spirituality.

   a. *As for the spiritual perfections they are man's birthright and belong to him alone of all creation. Man is, in reality, a spiritual being, and only when he lives in the spirit is he truly happy.*

   ('Abdu'l-Bahá, *Paris Talks*, 72)

   b. *The fountain of divine generosity it is gushing forth, but we must have thirst for the living waters. Unless there be thirst, the salutary water will not assuage. Unless the soul hungers, the delicious foods of the heavenly table will not give sustenance. Unless the eyes of perception be opened, the lights of the sun will not be witnessed. Until the nostrils are purified, the fragrance of the divine rose garden will not be inhaled. Unless the heart be filled with longing the favors of the Lord will not be evident....If an ocean of salubrious water is surging and we be not thirsty, what benefit do we receive? If the candle be lighted and we have no eyes, what enjoyment do we obtain from it? If melodious anthems should rise to the heavens and we are bereft of hearing, what enjoyment can we find?*

   ('Abdu'l-Bahá, *Promulgation of Universal Peace*, talk dated June 16, 1912)

   c. *It is not sufficient for a believer merely to accept and observe the teachings. He should, in addition, cultivate the sense of spirituality which he can acquire chiefly by means of prayer.*

   (from a letter written on behalf of Shoghi Effendi, in Hornby, *Lights of Guidance*, 506)

   d. *It is good for the Bahá'ís to learn that being a Bahá'í is essentially an inner thing, or way of life, and not dependent on fixed patterns.*

   (from a letter written on behalf of Shoghi Effendi in Hornby, *Lights of Guidance*, 77)

7. Be patient with myself.

   a. *We must not only be patient with others, infinitely patient, but also*

with our own poor selves, remembering that even the Prophets of
God sometimes got tired and cried out in despair!

(Shoghi Effendi, *Unfolding Destiny*, 456)

   b. "Perfectionism is self-abuse of the highest order."

(Anne Wilson Schaef, in Breathnach,
Simple Abundance, May 15).

8. Identify small things which make me happy.

   a. *All that which ye potentially possess can, however, be manifested only as a result of your own volition.*

(Bahá'u'lláh, *Gleanings*, 149)

   b. *The first Taráz and the first effulgence which hath dawned from the horizon of the Mother Book is that man should know his own self and recognize that which leadeth unto loftiness or lowliness, glory or abasement, wealth or poverty.*

(Bahá'u'lláh, *Tablets of Bahá'u'lláh*, 34–35)

9. Practice laughing and smiling.

   a. *May everyone point to you and ask, "Why are these people so happy?" I want you to be happy…to laugh, smile and rejoice in order that others may be made happy by you. I will pray for you.*

('Abdu'l-Bahá, *Promulgation of Universal Peace*, 218)

   b. *Laugh and talk, don't lament and talk. Laugh and speak. Laughter is caused by the slackening or relaxation of the nerves. It is an ideal condition and not physical. Laughter is the visible effect of an invisible cause. For example, happiness and misery are super-sensuous phenomenon. One cannot hear them with his ears or touch them with his hands. Happiness is a spiritual state.…This is the day of happiness. In no time of any manifestation was there the cause for happiness as now. A happy state brings special blessings. When the mind is depressed, the blessings are not received.*

('Abdu'l-Bahá, *Star of the West*, Vol. 8, 102)

10. When I catch myself being unhappy, worried, miserable, depressed, I can ask myself, "How am I making myself unhappy

right now?" This is not about blaming myself; it is about the gift of empowerment, which comes with taking responsibility.

    a. *Beware, lest thou allow anything whatsoever to grieve thee.*

        (Bahá'u'lláh, *Gleanings*, 303)

    b. *Let not the happenings of the world sadden you.*

        (Shoghi Effendi, *Advent of Divine Justice*, 82)

11. Remind myself that numbness is not a feeling; it is a state of refusal to acknowledge feelings. Our Creator has given us our feeling so that we can more fully enjoy life, be responsive to it and be able to responsibly take care of ourselves. Our Exemplar, 'Abdu'l-Bahá, expressed emotions freely.

    a. Dr. Zia Baghdádí recalled 'Abdu'l-Bahá's response to this prayer revealed by Bahá'u'lláh in Sulamáníyyih: "Create in me a pure heart…" That response? "When for the first time I read this tablet, I wept openly" (as cited in Furútan, *Stories of Bahá'u'lláh*, 20).

    b. I have heard stories from individuals that the Master laughed wholeheartedly and even danced with joy.

12. I can celebrate any and all progress.

    a. *They have not properly understood that man's supreme honor and real happiness lie in self-respect, in high resolves and noble purposes, in integrity and moral quality, in immaculacy of mind.*

        ('Abdu'l-Bahá, *Secret of Divine Civilization*, 19)

    b. In response to a believer who had asked how she could transform herself, 'Abdu'l-Bahá responded, "little by little, day by day."

        ('Abdu'l-Bahá, in *The Bahá'í World Vol. 12*, 706)

13. I can celebrate noticing setbacks and identify them as a "growing edge."

    a. *Let each morn be better than its eve and each morrow richer than its yesterday.*

        (Bahá'u'lláh, *Tablets of Bahá'u'lláh*, 138)

    b. (Fafar here!) The first step in the process of spiritual transformation is identification of what needs to be changed.

Therefore, acknowledging our shortcomings and resolving to transform them are in and of themselves worthy of celebration.

14. Remind myself that it is often my interpretation of external events that makes me unhappy and keeps me that way.

    a. *Although the bestowal is great and the grace is glorious, yet capacity and readiness are requisite. Without capacity and readiness, the divine bounty will not become manifest and evident. No matter how much the cloud may rain, the sun may shine and the breezes blow, the soil that is sterile will give no growth. The ground that is pure and free from thorns and thistles receives and produces through the rain of the cloud of mercy. No matter how much the sun shines, it will have no effect upon the black rock, but in a pure and polished mirror its lights become resplendent. Therefore, we must develop capacity in order that the signs of the mercy of the Lord may be revealed in us. We must endeavor to free the soil of the hearts from useless weeds and sanctify it from the thorns of worthless thoughts in order that the cloud of mercy may bestow its power upon us.*

       ('Abdu'l-Bahá, *Promulgation of Universal Peace*, 195)

    b. *Imagination is one of our greatest powers and a most difficult one to rule. Imagination is the father of superstition…we are led astray by imagination even in violation of will and reason. It is our test power. We are tested by our ability to control and subordinate it. Imagination is our greatest misleader. We hold to it until it becomes fixed in memory. Then we hold to it the stronger, believing it to be fact. It is a great power of the soul but without value unless rightly controlled and guided.*

       ('Abdu'l-Bahá, as cited in Grundy, *Ten Days in the Light of 'Akká*, 30)

    c. *It is good for the Bahá'ís to learn that being a Bahá'í is essentially an inner thing, or way of life, and not dependent on fixed patterns. Important as our organized institutions are, they are not the Faith itself. The strength of the Cause grows no matter how much disrupted its activities may temporarily be.*

       (from a letter written on behalf of Shoghi Effendi, in Hornby, *Lights of Guidance*, 77)

d. *And yet, how often we seem to forget the clear and repeated warning of our beloved Master, who in particular during the concluding years of His Mission on earth, laid stress on the severe mental tests that would inevitably sweep over His loved ones of the West...tests that would purge, purify and prepare them for their noble mission in life.*

(from a letter written by Shoghi Effendi, in Hornby, *Lights of Guidance*, 135)

15. Remind myself that transforming and improving my inner and outer character has a significant impact on the quality of my service and the ultimate victory of the Cause.

   a. *They have not properly understood that man's supreme honor and real happiness lie in self-respect, in high resolves and noble purposes, in integrity and moral quality, in immaculacy of mind.*

   ('Abdu'l-Bahá, *Secret of Divine Civilization*, 19)

   b. Bahá'ís should seek to be many-sided, normal and well-balanced, mentally and spiritually. We must not give the impression of being fanatics but at the same time we must live up to our principles.

   (letter written by the Universal House of Justice to an individual believer, in Hornby, *Lights of Guidance*, 112)

   c. *There is a difference between character and faith; it is often hard to accept this fact and put up with it, but the fact remains that a person may believe in and love the Cause – even being ready to die for it – and yet not have a good personal character or possess traits at variance with the teachings. We should try to change, to let the Power of God help recreate us and make us true Bahá'ís in deed as well as in belief. But the process is slow; sometimes it never happens because the individual does not try hard enough. But these things cause us suffering and are a test to us.*

   (quote from a letter written by Shoghi Effendi, in Hornby, *Lights of Guidance*, 76)

   d. Not by the force of numbers, not by the mere exposition of a set of new and noble principles, not by an organized campaign of teaching – no matter how worldwide and elaborate in its character – not even by the staunchness of our faith or the exaltation of our enthusiasm, can we ultimately hope to vindicate in the eyes of a critical and skeptical age the supreme claim of the Abhá Revelation. One thing and only one thing will unfailingly and alone secure the undoubted triumph of this sacred Cause, namely, the extent to which our own inner life and private character mirror forth in their manifold aspects the splendor of those eternal principles proclaimed by Bahá'u'lláh.

> (quote from a letter written on behalf of the Universal House of Justice, in Hornby, *Lights of Guidance*, 366)

16. Remind myself that I am more effective in whatever I do when I am joyful, whether it is meeting the challenges of daily life, serving the Cause in any capacity, or teaching the Faith.

Joy gives us wings! In times of joy our strength is more vital, our intellect keener, and our understanding less clouded. We seem better able to cope with the world and to find our sphere of usefulness.

> ('Abdu'l-Bahá, *Paris Talks*, 109)

17. Remind myself that ultimately, I am primarily responsible for one life — my own.

   a. *It follows, therefore, that every man hath been, and will continue to be, able of himself to appreciate the Beauty of God, the Glorified. Had he not been endowed with such a capacity; how could he be called to account for his failure? If, in the Day when all the peoples of the earth will be gathered together, any man should, whilst standing in the presence of God, be asked: "Wherefore hast thou disbelieved in My Beauty and turned away from My Self," and if such a man should reply and say: "Inasmuch as all men have erred, and none hath been found willing to turn his face to the Truth, I, too, following their example, have grievously failed to recognize the Beauty of the Eternal," such a plea will, assuredly, be rejected. For the faith of no man can be conditioned by anyone except himself.*

   > (Bahá'u'lláh, *Gleanings*, 143)

   b. *Each of us is responsible for one life only, and that is our own. Each of us is immeasurably far from being "perfect as our heavenly Father is perfect" and the task of perfecting our own life and character is one that requires all our attention, our will-power and energy. If we allow our attention and energy to be taken up in efforts to keep others right and remedy their faults, we are wasting precious time.*

(from a letter written on behalf of Shoghi Effendi, in Hornby, *Lights of Guidance*, 92)

c. *We often feel that our happiness lies in a certain direction; and yet, if we have to pay too heavy a price for it in the end we may discover that we have not really purchased either freedom or happiness, but just some new situation of frustration and disillusion.*

(from a letter written on behalf of Shoghi Effendi, in Hornby, *Lights of Guidance*, 393)

18. Refer to the "Owner's Manual" when I become confused about who I am and what the purpose of my life is.

   a. *O My servants! Could ye apprehend with what wonders of My munificence and bounty I have willed to entrust your souls, ye would, of a truth, rid yourselves of attachment to all created things, and would gain a true knowledge of your own selves — a knowledge which is the same as the comprehension of Mine own Being. Ye would find yourselves independent of all else but Me, and would perceive, with your inner and outer eye, and as manifest as the revelation of My effulgent Name, the seas of My loving-kindness and bounty moving within you.*

   (Bahá'u'lláh, *Gleanings*, 326)

   b. *Whatever duty Thou hast prescribed unto Thy servants of extolling to the utmost Thy majesty and glory is but a token of Thy grace unto them, that they may be enabled to ascend unto the station conferred upon their own inmost being, the station of the knowledge of their own selves.*

   (Bahá'u'lláh, *Gleanings*, 4)

   c. *O Son of Spirit! The best beloved of all things in My sight is Justice; turn not away therefrom if thou desirest Me, and neglect it not that I may confide in thee. By its aid thou shalt see with thine own eyes and not through the eyes of others, and shalt know of thine own knowledge and not through the knowledge of thy neighbour.*

   (Bahá'u'lláh, *Hidden Words*, 3)

d. *When one is released from the prison of self that is indeed freedom, for self is the greatest prison.*

('Abdu'l-Bahá, *'Abdu'l-Bahá in London*, 120)

e. *Regarding the points you refer to in your letter: the complete and entire elimination of the ego would imply perfection – which man can never completely attain – but the ego can and should be ever-increasingly subordinated to the enlightened soul of man.*

(from a letter written on behalf of Shoghi Effendi, "Living the Life," 11)

f. *If we could perceive the true reality of things we would see that the greatest of all battles raging in the world today is the spiritual battle. If the believers like yourself, young and eager and full of life, desire to win laurels for true and undying heroism, then let them join in the spiritual battle – whatever their physical occupation may be – which involves the very soul of man. The hardest and the noblest task in the world today is to be a true Bahá'í; this requires that we defeat not only the current evils prevailing all over the world, but the weaknesses, attachments to the past, prejudices, and selfishnesses that may be inherited and acquired within our own characters; that we give forth a shining and incorruptible example to our fellow-men.*

(from a letter written on behalf of Shoghi Effendi, in Universal House of Justice, *Compilation of Compilations*, Vol. 1, 381)

g. Not all believers can give public talks, not all are called upon to serve on administrative institutions. But all can pray, fight their own spiritual battles, and contribute to the Fund. If every believer will carry out these sacred duties, we shall be astonished at the accession of power which will result to the whole body, and which in its turn will give rise to further growth and the showering of greater blessings on all of us.

(September 1964 message to the Bahá'ís of the world, in Universal House of Justice, *Wellspring of Guidance*, 38)

19. Remind myself of the ephemeral nature of my physical life, which is less than a blink of an eye compared to a glorious eternity.

a. *The world is but a show, vain and empty, a mere nothing, having the resemblance of reality. Set not your affections upon it.*

(Bahá'u'lláh, *Gleanings*, 328; also, *Bahá'í World Faith*, 68)

b. *Sorrow not if, in these days and on this earthly plane, things contrary to your wishes have been ordained and manifested by God, for days of blissful joy, of heavenly delight, are assuredly in store for you.*

(Bahá'u'lláh, *Gleanings*, 329)

c. *Therefore, be ye rejoiced, for ye are sheltered beneath the providence of God. Be happy and joyous because the bestowals of God are intended for you and the life of the Holy Spirit is breathing upon you. Rejoice, for the heavenly table is prepared for you. Rejoice, for the angels of heaven are your assistants and helpers. Rejoice, for the glance of the Blessed Beauty, Bahá'u'lláh is directed upon you. Rejoice for Bahá'u'lláh is your Protector. Rejoice, for the glory everlasting is destined for you. Rejoice for the eternal life is awaiting you.*

('Abdu'l-Bahá, *Promulgation of Universal Peace*, 209)

Compiling this list has helped me bring some guidance and specificity toward the actualization of the mandate of being happy. I find it useful to revisit this list from time to time as a refresher for myself. My hope is that this list will do the same for you.

"What's Love Got to Do with It?"

Well, it seems like love has got everything to do with it, if "it" is everything in creation, including and above all, our Creator. These are just a few drops from the ocean of the Writings relating to "love." Let's start at the "cosmic" level:

> *Love is the most great law that ruleth this mighty and heavenly cycle, the unique power that bindeth together the divers elements of this material world, the supreme magnetic force that directeth the movements of the spheres in the celestial realms. Love revealeth with unfailing and limitless power the mysteries latent in the universe.* ('Abdu'l-Bahá, *Selections*, 320)

Wow, every time I read this passage, I feel excitement, awe, and wonder that even inanimate objects are influenced and regulated by the law of love. How pitifully limited my understanding of love has been! The silly thought popped into my head that "love is the Supreme Divine Superglue."

After being told that all of inanimate material existence is governed by the profound law of love, we now move to its vital impact on humanity.

> *Love is the spirit of life unto the adorned body of mankind, the establisher of true civilization in this mortal world, and the shedder of imperishable glory upon every high-aiming race and nation.* ('Abdu'l-Bahá, *Selections*, 27)

According to this verse, everything we know of our civilization—past, present, and future—has been governed by the power of love. God also addresses us at a more accessible, individual level:

> *…I knew My love for thee, hence I created thee. Wherefore do thou love Me that I may name thy name and fill thy soul with the spirit of life.*
>
> (Bahá'u'lláh, *Hidden Words*, 4)

Love is heaven's kindly light, the Holy Spirit's eternal breath that vivifies the human soul.

('Abdu'l-Bahá, in *The Bahá'í World Vol. 2*, 50)

Naturally, it follows that love is the common foundation of all religions: "There is nothing greater or more blessed than the Love of God! The essence of all religions is the Love of God, and it is the foundation of all the sacred teachings" ('Abdu'l-Bahá, *Paris Talks*, 82). Love's role and impact are not limited to this ephemeral, material existence, either: "Love is the one means that ensureth true felicity in this world and the next" ('Abdu'l-Bahá, *Selections*, 12).

Then, there are innumerable mandates in the Writings, as there are within the holy scriptures of all religions, relative to how love should inform and regulate our behavior toward each other:

If any differences arise amongst you, behold me standing before your face, and overlook the faults of one another for My name's sake...

(Bahá'u'lláh, *Tablets of Bahá'u'lláh*, 315)

Be as a lamp unto them that walk in darkness, a joy to the sorrowful...

(Bahá'u'lláh, *Gleanings*, 285)

Blessed is he who preferreth his brother before himself.

(Bahá'u'lláh, *Tablets of Bahá'u'lláh*, 71)

Surely, when we realize how God loves and cares for us, we should so order our lives that we may become more like Him.

('Abdu'l-Bahá, *Paris Talks*, 120)

Love is the fundamental principle of God's purpose for man, and He has commanded us to love each other even as He loves us.

('Abdu'l-Bahá, *Paris Talks*, 122)

Never become angry with one another....Love the creatures for the sake of God and not for themselves. You will never become angry or impatient if you love them for the sake of God.

('Abdu'l-Bahá, *Promulgation of Universal Peace*, 93)

...for man can receive no greater gift than this, that he rejoice another's heart.

('Abdu'l-Bahá, *Selections*, 203–4)

So far, so good. Through a cursory sampling of the Writings, we have established that love is the greatest law of the universe, the very cause for our creation; we are called to emulate God by loving each other. We arrive at a potential dilemma, however, when it comes to loving ourselves: the Writings are full of frightening admonitions concerning self-love.

Burst thy cage asunder....Renounce thyself...

(Bahá'u'lláh, *Tablets of Bahá'u'lláh*, 118)

O Son of Man! If thou lovest Me, turn away from thyself, and if thou seekest My pleasure, regard not thine own, that thou mayest die in Me and I may eternally live in thee.

(Bahá'u'lláh, *Hidden Words*, 5)

Forget your own selves, and turn your eyes towards your neighbor.

(Bahá'u'lláh, *Gleanings*, 9)

The station of absolute self-surrender transcendeth, and will ever remain exalted above, every other station.

(Bahá'u'lláh, *Tablets of Bahá'u'lláh*, 338)

...give up thy self that thou mayest find the Peerless One...

(Bahá'u'lláh, *The Seven Valleys*, 9)

...come forth from the sheath of self and desire that thy worth may be made resplendent...

(Bahá'u'lláh, *Hidden Words*, 47)

When one is released from the prison of self, that is indeed freedom! For self is the greatest prison.

('Abdu'l-Bahá, *Divine Art of Living*, 70)

If our chalice is full of self, there is no room in it for the water of life.

('Abdu'l-Bahá, *Paris Talks*, 136)

The "Master-Key" to self-mastery is self-forgetting.

('Abdu'l-Bahá, *Star of the West, Vol. 17*, 348)

...he should not seek out anything whatever for his own self in this swiftly-passing life...he should cut the self away...

('Abdu'l-Bahá, *Paris Talks*, 54)

These are just a few samplings of the daunting admonitions about self-love. Faced with these warnings, many of us seem to ignore and overlook our dual nature. We do have our material self, which is all that we share with the animal kingdom. Animals live by instinct alone; they are programmed to eat, procreate, fight if necessary, protect their young, and so on. If they kill, it is for survival—either to feed themselves or protect their territory. They have no choice in these matters.

We, on the other hand, have been told that we have a mind and intelligence far superior to animals. We have been endowed with the power to make choices; additionally, we have a soul and higher self that has been created in the image of God. It all comes down to the choices we make—and those choices are not always good, a fact verified by many tragic events.

Our task and challenge, given our dual nature, is to be constantly vigilant of the promptings of our lower nature, and to train and guide it with our higher nature. This higher self or nature is gifted with potentialities to exhibit all the virtues and attributes of God. How else could we make sense of this statement by Bahá'u'lláh?

> *O My servants! Could ye apprehend with what wonders of My munificence and bounty I have willed to entrust your souls, ye would, of a truth, rid yourselves of attachment to all created things, and would gain a true knowledge of your own selves – a knowledge which is the same as the comprehension of Mine Own Being. Ye would find yourselves independent of all else but Me, and would perceive, with your inner and outer eye, and as manifest as the revelation of My Effulgent Name, the seas of My loving-kindness and bounty moving within you. (Gleanings, 326-27)*

The dire warnings and admonitions against self-love are about a self that is completely cut off from their higher, potentially God-like self, one that is solely ruled by their lower nature. Bereft of the knowledge of who they are created to be, that person will live in an abyss of darkness and ignorance. Mr. Adib Taherzadeh, in his introduction to *The Covenant of Bahá'u'lláh*, elucidates that the world of nature reflects many spiritual realities. He compares the duality of human nature to a tree, which must be rooted in the soil for its sustenance even as it is programmed to grow upward and bask in the sun's life-giving rays. If the tree had the power of choice and made the decision to not grow up, it would have failed its very reason for being—to become a tree. He continues this metaphor by stating that as human beings in this earthly life, we are rooted in the material world for our physical survival; however, our created purpose is to reach heavenward, to fulfill our destiny as spiritual beings. Unlike the tree, we have been endowed with the ability to make choices, which is potentially a perilous gift: we can busy ourselves with the material side of life to the point of ignoring and neglecting the very purpose for our creation, which is to develop our spiritual side. The dire warnings in the Writings against self-love refer to the self that has made the choice to regard themselves as the center of their universe. I once heard Mr. Hooper Dunbar's talk, in which he compared our dual nature to that of a horse and its rider. The horse symbolizes our lower nature; the rider represents our higher self. The rider's task is to train and gain mastery over the horse, so that he can guide it to where he wants it to go. If the untrained horse is in charge of its rider, a potentially disastrous situation arises.

Personally, I deeply appreciate the above analogy. To me, it suggests the necessity of a collaborative relationship between our higher and lower natures. The rider has to lovingly and patiently train the horse; he should not be abusive toward the animal in the name of training. In fact, when 'Abdu'l-Bahá was asked about physical punishment of children, his response was that we should not strike a child (*Selections*, 95).

From observation of myself and many other Bahá'ís in the context of workshops or individual/group therapy, I have come to the conclusion that many of us have become self-abusive in response, or in reaction, to the warnings about self-love. It is as if we believe that the more we ignore or neglect ourselves, the more we must be in tune with the Writings. Some of us from other religious backgrounds are already burdened with a heavy load of inherited guilt (i.e., the concept of original sin). I think it is easy to do a real number on our poor selves by adding this inheritance to the warnings in the Writings.

I find this passage from 'Abdu'l-Bahá illuminating:

> *With reference to what is meant by an individual becoming entirely forgetful of self: the intent is that he should rise up and sacrifice himself in the true sense, that is he should obliterate the promptings of the human condition, and rid himself of such characteristics as are worthy of blame and constitute the gloomy darkness of this life on earth — not that he should allow his physical health to deteriorate and his body to become infirm. (Selections, 180)*

In fact, I think another tendency of ours—perhaps because we want to be on the safe side—is to lump our two selves together and become an equal opportunity self-abuser! When this happens, I think we have failed to "translate that which hath been written into reality and action" (Bahá'u'lláh, *Gleanings*, 250). We seem to have all but forgotten what Bahá'u'lláh says: "Be fair to yourselves and to others, that the evidences of justice may be revealed, through your deeds, among Our faithful servants"

(*Gleanings*, 278). This passage informs me that my service to humanity will be more effective when I start by being fair to myself.

In general, I think that many of us are too hard on ourselves in nonproductive, dysfunctional ways. We seem to evince an attitude that says "if I don't like myself and ignore my wants and needs, I am obeying God" (or "I am being a good Bahá'í"). It is dysfunctional—by being unfair to myself, I become despondent and non-productive. Instead of exuding genuine spiritual contentment and happiness, in order that others may be made happy [by me], I may become bitter and critical of those who truly like themselves and spontaneously like others as well. Here, we arrive once more at the need to assuming a loving, attentive, encouraging, and patient position as we engage in our own process of spiritual transformation. I cannot dislike—or worse, hate—myself and hope to acquire virtues and attributes. Nowhere in the Writings do I find a program of self-abuse as a model for spiritual transformation!

At this moment, it might be helpful to candidly focus on our own inner dialogue with our selves, and see how it compares with what the Writings advocate. Although some of the following passages primarily address our treatment of others, I think we could safely assume that we, too, can consider ourselves "others" in our self-dialogues.

> *Look not upon the creatures of God except with the eye of kindliness and of mercy, for Our loving providence hath pervaded all created things, and Our grace encompasseth the earth and the heavens.*
>
> (Bahá'u'lláh, *Gleanings*, 33)

> *Show forbearance and benevolence and love to one another.*
>
> (Bahá'u'lláh, *Gleanings*, 8)

> *Hear no evil, and see no evil, abase not thyself...*
>
> (Bahá'u'lláh, *Hidden Words*, 12)

> *Be ye careful and bring not despondency upon any soul.*
>
> (The Báb, *Selections*, 141)

> *...ever strive for gentleness and love.*
>
> ('Abdu'l-Bahá, *Tablets of 'Abdu'l-Bahá Abbás*, 656–57)

> *...those who are barbed of claw should turn gentle and forbearing...*
>
> ('Abdu'l-Bahá, *Selections*, 11)

...strive to gladden every soul.

('Abdu'l-Bahá, *Divine Art of Living*, 55)

...man's supreme honor and real happiness lie in self-respect...

('Abdu'l-Bahá, *Secret of Divine Civilization*, 19)

I find the following passage especially illuminating in terms of how we inwardly address ourselves and our shortcomings: "Refrain from reprimanding them, and if you wish to give admonition or advice, let it be offered in such a way that it will not burden the hearer" ('Abdu'l-Bahá, *Promulgation of Universal Peace*, 453). So, if I inwardly call myself unbecoming names and am I mercilessly critical of my flaws, I am essentially ignoring God's guidance of the power of utterance.

The Great Being saithe: Human utterance is an essence which aspireth to exert its influence and needeth moderation....As to its moderation, this hath to be combined with tact and wisdom... (Bahá'u'lláh, *Tablets of Bahá'u'lláh*, 62)

The following passage could be an analogy for the process of spiritual transformation:

Moderation is necessary in all affairs. Man must take a lesson from divine actions and deeds for God suffers a tree to grow a long time before it attains to perfection. He is able to make a tree grow to fruition in an instant, but wisdom requires a gradual development. ('Abdu'l-Bahá, *Selections*, 26)

We know that perfection is an impossible goal to achieve for human beings; nonetheless, we are instructed to perfect our characters. The above passage informs me that it is a gradual process that requires moderation.

Many of us, however, seem to have inner barriers when it comes to being fair and kind to ourselves. Artist and author Julia Cameron makes the following observation: "Any little experimenting in self-nurturance is very frightening for most of us" (in Breathnach, *Simple Abundance*, March 15). Additionally, I recently heard author Elizabeth Gilbert on the radio program *On Being...with Krista Tippet* ("Elizabeth Gilbert: Choosing Curiosity Over Fear"). During the program, the topic of how we treat ourselves came up. Gilbert stated that she had finally made peace with all her "selves." She added that for most of us the notion of "self-love" may be too charged and intimidating; she suggested that being "friendly with self" may be more palatable. I find this framing more in harmony with the notions of "fairness" and "self-respect" mentioned in The Writings. When we relate to our higher self, which is created potentially in the image of

God, we can truly love and honor that self; when we approach this higher self with love and respect, we are really loving and honoring the divine virtues and attributes within us. So, in a way, we love God by loving and nurturing the potentially God-like attributes within us, and then using our particular gifts and talents in service to humanity.

I would like to finish this section with the account of the encounter between Howard Colby Ives, at the time a Unitarian minister, and 'Abdu'l-Bahá during his visit to the United States in 1912.

> *Then we sat in the two chairs by the window: knee to knee, eye to eye. At last He looked right into me. It was the first time since our eyes had met with His first beckoning gesture that this had happened. And now nothing intervened between us and He looked at me. He looked at me! It seemed as though never before had anyone really seen me. I felt a sense of gladness that I at last was at home, and that one who knew me utterly, my Father, in truth, was alone with me.*
>
> *As He looked such play of thought found reflection in His face, that if He had talked an hour not nearly so much could have been said. A little surprise, perhaps, followed swiftly by such sympathy, such understanding, such overwhelming love – it was as if His very being opened to receive me. With that the heart within me melted and the tears flowed. I did not weep, in any ordinary sense. There was no breaking up of feature. It was as if a long-pent stream was at last undammed. Unheeded, as I looked at Him, they flowed.*
>
> *He put His two thumbs to my eyes while He wiped the tears from my face; admonishing me not to cry, that one must always be happy. And He laughed. Such a ringing, boyish laugh. It was as though He had discovered the most delightful joke imaginable: a divine joke which only He could appreciate.*
>
> *I could not speak. We both sat perfectly silent for what seemed a long while, and gradually a great peace came to me. Then 'Abdu'l-Bahá placed His hand upon my breast saying that it was the heart that speaks.*
>
> *Again silence: a long, heart-enthralling silence. No word further was spoken, and all the time I was with Him not one single sound came from me. But no word was necessary from me to Him. I knew that, even then, and how I thanked God it was so.*
>
> *Suddenly He leaped from His chair with another laugh as though consumed with a heavenly joy. Turning, He took me under the elbows and lifted me to my feet and swept me into his arms. Such a hug! No mere embrace! My very ribs cracked. He kissed me on both cheeks, laid His arm across my shoulders and led me to the door.*
>
> *That is all. But life has never been quite the same since.* (Portals to Freedom, 32–33)

Oh, would that we could see ourselves and each other through the loving, forgiving, and soul-penetrating eyes of 'Abdu'l-Bahá!

Afterword

Some of the people who had graciously agreed to read my unfinished manuscript, in addition to sharing some insightful suggestions, also commented that the book had started on a personal note and should perhaps end on one. So, I decided to add this afterword.

In the main text, I did not mention that I have had two bouts with breast cancer. The first one was in 2009, and I received surgery and radiation around the time when our son was going through his traumatic experiences. In retrospect, I see that my thoughts and feelings were so consumed with him that my cancer experience was totally on the back burner; I basically went through the motions of dealing with it — with a lot of loving support from family and loyal friends, of course.

The second cancer episode was in 2014, when the same cancer showed up in my spine, which evidently was fortuitous since it caused excruciating back pain. After several weeks of failed attempts to find the cause of the pain, we ended up in the ER, where the diagnosis of the return of the breast cancer was made. So, we were deeply grateful to hear from my oncologist that had it not been for the extreme pain, the cancer could have spread without any other outer symptoms. I praised God for the pain and proceeded to have radiation, which killed the cancer but also fractured two of my lower vertebrae. To fix the fractures, I had to undergo two back surgeries and was put on highly addictive pain medicines for about 10 months. Getting off these meds, as necessary as they may have been, was unexpectedly challenging and somewhat traumatic. Although my experience was nothing but a glimpse into the struggle of addiction, I developed deep sympathy for people who fight to overcome various forms of addictions. In summary: parts of 2014 and 2015 were quite challenging.

In late May 2015, deeply moved by the overwhelming show of love and support in response to Facebook updates ceaselessly posted by my beloved Minou, I decided to post the final update. I include that post here, verbatim, since that too was part of my journey.

Physical health update:

A. As far as the cancer goes, I am in remission! According to my oncologist, the cancer will likely return; it could be within 6 months to a year, or 5 years or longer. I am to have a PET scan once every 6 months to monitor the situation.

B. My back surgery is considered a success; the pain and discomfort are now quite tolerable. I am off of all narcotic pain meds except the Fentanyl patch, which will gradually be reduced until I no longer need it.

C. I continue to live with Chronic Fatigue Syndrome, now in its 18th year. This is a challenging mind, body, and soul-crushing experience on bad days, which makes me infinitely grateful for the good days. This takes a lot of my life energy. This is also the reason for my inability to respond to your kind and loving sentiments expressed in so many ways. Please forgive me and know that I would if I could, and that in my heart and soul I am eternally grateful.

Mental, emotional and spiritual update:

The outpouring of love and prayers for me, and my family, in the early months of my cancer journey is what enabled me to face the increasingly more difficult challenges that lay ahead! At this early phase, I felt seen, heard and loved by God and all of you, His lovely creation. In the later phases, as I was feeling that I had exhausted all my magnificent support system (of course this was totally in my head; there was no indication from my loving family or loyal friends to warrant my negative feelings) was also when the crises seemed to become relentless. It was during this phase that my spirits started to plummet and I went to what we call in some therapeutic circles as my "favorite unpleasant feeling" place. For me this place is characterized by dark, lonely feelings and thoughts like "God doesn't really love me" and/or "I am being punished for something(s) I did in the past, or many good things that I haven't done enough of," etc., etc. This for me is the definition of a "Hellish place," when I feel disconnected from God and Bahá'u'lláh. And of course, "Heaven" for me is when I feel that deep, intimate, loving connection to Bahá'u'lláh. There is no sweeter place, therefore remoteness from it is pure torture. Of course, intellectually I was aware of one of my favorite Hidden Words, "My calamity is my providence, outwardly it is fire and vengeance and inwardly it is light and mercy." I knew that I was only in touch with the calamitous "fire and vengeance," "providence, light and mercy" seemed remote and unattainable. I tried to remind myself of past personal tests and difficulties, that I needed to be patient and surrender to what was, even though I may not understand it. In the past I have even said humorously, "Okay God, I feel the fire and vengeance, now please show me the money! (I'm ready for some light and mercy!)

My "higher self" worked hard to remind me that God has always been faithful to His word and that sometimes within a few months or as long as many years later, I would understand the purpose or wisdom of a particular test and become the humble recipient of its particular gifts. However, my "lower self" was not buying it. I often found myself revisiting and consoled by the passage from the Guardian that says, "ultimately all the battle of life is within the individual" (Shoghi Effendi, "Living the Life," 12).

Though the return to "normal" or routine life has felt painfully slow, I am happy to report the resumption of my two bi-monthly therapy groups last month. I have led therapy groups for the past 27 years and they have been a significant and joyful part of my life.

As for what I am looking forward to: 1. The celebration of 50 years of marriage to my sweetheart, Jack Guillebeaux, and the creation of our loving supportive family. Throughout our 50-year journey with its inevitable ups and downs, I have personally come to appreciate the Divine institution of marriage as the ideal crucible for spiritual growth and development. 2. The other goal is finishing my book tentatively entitled *Spiritual Transformation; Reclaiming Our Birthright*. Over 20 years ago, the outline for this project was praised by the Universal House of Justice. This feels like my life's work: bringing together the overarching and lofty guidance from the Writings and combining it with practical tools of psychotherapy in order to facilitate spiritual transformation. And it is in this area that I once again humbly feel emboldened to ask for your prayers and spiritual support, that is if I have not completely used up my quota. ;-)

Words really cannot express the depth of my soul's gratitude for each and every prayer, thought, encouragement, pictures, jokes, gifts, cards, calls and visits over this past year. I'm sending virtual hugs and kisses to you all.

Fafar, 2015

It has been five years since I wrote the above update. As I mentioned, I was then looking forward to our 50th anniversary. So, while I was staying at Minou and Rob's, going through some of the worst symptoms of withdrawal from prescribed opioids, our daughters and son, with great support from Kim and Julian, were busily planning the most fabulous 50th anniversary celebration for us. I was still quite out of it and unable to be of any assistance to them. My only job was to go shopping with my lovely friend of 40 years, Arefeh Partovi Langkilde, in Atlanta—where we found a beautiful dress to which Arefeh skillfully made the necessary alterations. It was a glorious celebration of our 50-year marriage as well as a well-timed culmination of a difficult year.

As to the second goal mentioned in the update, I am happy and grateful to report that my book is finally finished! I am now in the process of adding some finishing touches, such as this afterword. So, now I am looking forward to its publication. My highest wish now is that after publication, the book might reach anyone who could benefit from it.

As to my physical health, I continue to have a PET scan every six months to check on the status of the dormant cancer; so far, so good! I am happy to report that I am only very minimally anxious as I go for the PET scans. My basic stance of detachment is that if and when the cancer returns we will, with the help of God, deal with it the best way we can.

At 77 I am now in the 22nd year of CFS, which continues to be a challenge; nonetheless, by it is now a familiar one. There, again, I work at maintaining a stance of acceptance and resignation, even as I continue to partake of necessary treatments of IVs and supplements. So, as I look back on the entirety of my life, I see a series of crises followed by victories and numerous unearned blessings. What I mean by "victories" are my efforts to comprehend and glean any shred of insight and wisdom inherent in the experience of any particular crisis, and then sharing it with those who might be interested. My approach to any issue big or small is to engage in practical problem solving as well as in total reliance on God for what He would consider the best solution and outcome. I find this to be an ongoing journey of a relationship with my Creator.

At this point two passages, one from a poem by Rumi, and the other from the Writings of Bahá'u'lláh, are what express both my stance toward life and my highest wishes for myself.

The Guest House

This being human is a guest house.
Every morning a new arrival.

A joy, a depression, a meanness,
some momentary awareness comes
as an unexpected visitor.

Welcome and entertain them all!
Even if they're a crowd of sorrows,
who violently sweep your house
empty of its furniture,
still, treat each guest honorably.
He may be clearing you out
for some new delight.

The dark thought, the shame, the malice,
meet them at the door laughing,

and invite them in.

Be grateful for whoever comes,
because each has been sent
as a guide from beyond.

— Rumi

"The Guest House" from *The Illuminated Rumi* by Jalal Al-Din Rumi, translated by Coleman Barks, copyright © 1997 by Coleman Barks and Michael Green. Used by permission of Broadway Books, an imprint of Random House, a division of Penguin Random House LLC. All rights reserved.

    I have experienced firsthand the truth and wisdom enshrined in this mystical poem. So often, in what I feared, resisted, or fought against, lay the kernel of a major divine blessing, seemingly unattainable, except through a crisis.

Therefore, what I am left with is best expressed through these words of Bahá'u'lláh:

I beg of Thee, O my God, by Thy most exalted Word which Thou hast ordained as the Divine Elixir unto all who are in Thy realm, the Elixir through whose potency the crude metal of human life hath been transmuted into purest gold, O Thou in Whose hands are both the visible and invisible kingdoms, to ordain that my choice be conformed to Thy choice and my wish to Thy wish, that I may be entirely content with that which Thou didst desire, and be wholly satisfied with what Thou didst destine for me by Thy bounteousness and favor. Potent art Thou to do as Thou willest. Thou, in very truth, art the All-Glorious, the All-Wise.

(Bahá'u'lláh, *Prayers and Meditations*, 53)

Appendix

Acknowledgements

I acknowledge with joy, pleasure and deep gratitude:

My many clients and especially my long-term Group participants: over the past 30 years through their (own) commitment to the process of personal growth and transformation have provided me with an ongoing laboratory to experiment with perfecting my craft. A sincere "thanks" to you—you know who you are—for your trust in me and in the process.

My many friends and participants in my workshops, in Bahá'í and not- Bahá'í settings, who urged me to "put this stuff down in a book."

VISIONS—Vigorous InterventionS In Ongoing Natural Settings—for their permission to use some of the significant concepts developed by them.

My nearest and dearest, who through their own challenges or tests and difficulties provided me with ample opportunities to face and address my own shortcomings, and who generously permitted me to share part of their stories in this book. Thank you for your commitments to the process; we have grown together.

Annie Janus, herself a counselor, who lovingly volunteered to type the manuscript, braving my often-illegible handwriting as well as providing insightful feedback. I have immensely enjoyed our spiritual and joyful collaborative process; thanks, dearest Annie!

My late brilliant mentor, trainer, colleague, and friend, the late Dr. Josephine B. Lewis, from whom I was privileged to learn the science and art of doing therapy. You are still a source of inspiration to me.

Beloved Dr. Peter Kahn, who upon hearing my plans to write such a book, encouraged and urged me to submit an outline to the Universal House of Justice for its perusal. I would not have dared to do this on my own.

Julian MacQueen, for the whole-hearted support and generous hospitality in providing me an oasis of isolation and tranquility in his beachfront hotels to develop and pursue this project.

To the friend of my heart and soul, Kim MacQueen, who has not only blessed me with the gift of her friendship for the past 30-plus years but has also been a primary motivator and loving supporter of this project. It is not an exaggeration to say that I could not or would not have done this without you! So many times, when I was ready to give up, questioning the very validity of the task or my capacity to fulfill it; you disarmed me with your loving and often humorous interventions, helping me to get back on track. My very soul thanks you!

Finally, Jack Guillebeaux, who saw and honored potentialities in me long before I was aware of them. Thank you for whole-heartedly, and often sacrificially, supporting whatever endeavor I have chosen to pursue in the past 55 years. You are my rock.

Central Figures of the Bahá'í Faith

As Bahá'ís we consider ourselves, and by extension all humanity, especially fortunate to be living so close in time to the three Central Figures of the Bahá'í Faith, the Báb, Bahá'u'lláh, and 'Abdu'l-Bahá.

The Báb (1819–1850; The Gate) is a symbolic title of Siyyid Ali-Muhammad, the inaugurator of the Bahá'í Dispensation. Although an independent Messenger or Manifestation of God, the primary purpose of His mission was to serve as the Gate through which Bahá'u'lláh was introduced to humanity.

Bahá'u'lláh (1817–1892; The Glory of God): Mirza Husayn-Ali, also known by other titles such as The Ancient Beauty, the Blessed Beauty, the Word, the Wronged One, whom Bahá'ís believe to be the Promised One of all the former Dispensations, and has Revealed Teachings and laws to guide humanity for at least the next thousand years.

'Abdu'l-Bahá (1844–1921; the Servant of Baha or Glory) is the eldest son of Bahá'u'lláh (by the name of Abbás), whom Bahá'u'lláh appointed as His Successor and the Center of the Covenant, and bestowed with the authority to interpret Bahá'u'lláh's Writings. 'Abdu'l-Bahá holds a unique station of being the Perfect Exemplar of Bahá'u'lláh's principles and teachings. 'Abdu'l-Bahá in His Last Will and Testament appointed His grandson, Shoghi Effendi, as the "Guardian of the Faith."

The Guardian is Shoghi Effendi Rabbání (1897–1957). 'Abdu'l-Bahá refers to him as "The sign of God, the Chosen Branch, the Guardian of the Cause of God, he unto whom all must turn" (*Will and Testament of 'Abdu'l-Bahá*, 5). The Guardian's chief functions were to interpret the Writings of Bahá'u'lláh, the Báb, and 'Abdu'l-Bahá, and to establish the system of local and national Spiritual Assemblies around the world as a foundation for the eventual election of the Universal House of Justice.

The Universal House of Justice (1963–continuous). 'Abdu'l-Bahá established the Guardianship as a hereditary office; however, Shoghi

Effendi had no children, and therefore no successor could be appointed. Upon the Guardian's death in 1957, the Hands of the Cause of God—spiritually eminent believers named by Shoghi Effendi as the Faith's chief stewards—guided and protected the Faith until the election of the first Universal House of Justice in 1963.

The Universal House of Justice, as the head of the Bahá'í Administrative Order whose blueprint was established in the Writings of Bahá'u'lláh, is the supreme governing and legislative body of the Bahá'í Faith. Ordained by Bahá'u'lláh, its purpose is to ensure the continuity of divine guidance, to safeguard the unity of the Faith, and to maintain the integrity and flexibility of its Teachings. Bahá'ís are to obey all the decisions of the Universal House of Justice. 'Abdu'l-Bahá explains that whatever the Universal House of Justice decides "has the same effect as the Text itself" ('Abdu'l-Bahá, in Universal House of Justice, *Compilation of Compilations*, Vol. 2, 326)

As the Head of the Bahá'í Faith, the Universal House of Justice has nine members who are elected once every five years by the members of the National Spiritual Assemblies around the world at an international convention. National Spiritual Assemblies are administrative bodies annually elected by the Bahá'ís in each country. The Seat of the Universal House of Justice is located at the Bahá'í World Center on Mount Carmel in Haifa, Israel.

For more information about the history, Teachings, administrative order, and Bahá'ís around the world, please refer to www.bahai.org.

Suggested Reading List

Although the following books have not been directly used in the manuscript, they have in many ways deeply inspired my thinking and informed my soul. I list them here for your own explorations.

Al-Anon Family Groups. *Courage to Change: One Day at a Time in Al-Anon II*. Virginia Beach: Publisher's Cataloging in Publication, 1992.

Beattie, Melody. *Co-dependent No More*. Center City, MN: Hazelden, 1986.

Bender, Sue. *Everyday Sacred: A Woman's Journey Home*. San Francisco: Harper, 1995.

Borysenko, Joan. *Minding the Body, Mending the Mind*. Reading, MA: Addison-Wesley, 1984.

Chödrön, Pema. *Start Where You Are: A Guide to Compassionate Living*. Boston: Shambhala, 2001.

Chödrön, Pema. *When Things Fall Apart: Heart Advice for Difficult Times*. London: Shambhala, 2000.

Dobbs, Happy. *Spiritual Being: A User's Guide*. Oxford: George Ronald, 1997.

Dyer, Wayne W. *There's a Spiritual Solution to Every Problem*. New York: HarperCollins, 2001.

Hatcher, John S. *The Purpose of Physical Reality*. Wilmette, IL: Bahá'í Publishing, 1987.

Hay, Louise L. *You Can Heal Your Life*. Carson, CA: Hay House, 1984.

Hetzel, Rattana. *The Destiny of Women Is the Destiny of the World*. Palo Alto: Heart Quest Foundation, 1996.

Honnold, Annamarie, comp. *Divine Therapy: Pearls of Wisdom from the Bahá'í Writings*. Oxford: George Ronald, 1986.

Johnson, Lynn D. *Enjoy Life! Healing with Happiness*. Head Acre Publishing, 2008.

McGraw, Patricia Romano. *Seeking the Wisdom of the Heart: Reflections on Seven Stages of Spiritual Development*. Wilmette, IL: Bahá'í Publishing, 2007.

Moore, Thomas. *Care of the Soul: A Guide for Cultivating Depth and Sacredness in Everyday Life*. New York: Harper Perennial, 1992.

Motlagh, Hushidar. *The Glorious Journey to God: Selections from Sacred Scriptures on the Afterlife*. Mt. Pleasant, MI: Global Perspectives, 1994.

Popov, Linda Kavelin. *A Pace of Grace: The Virtues of a Sustainable Life*. New York: Penguin, 2004.

Rosen, Sidney, ed. *My Voice Will Go with You: The Teachings of Milton H. Erickson*. New York: W. W. Norton, 1982.

Schaef, Anne Wilson. *Women's Reality: An Emerging Female System in a White Male Society*. San Francisco: Harper & Row, 1981.

St. Rain, Justice. *Falling into Grace: The Trials and Triumphs of Becoming a Bahá'í*. Special Ideas, 1991.

Tolle, Eckhart. *A New Earth, Awakening to Your Life's Purpose*. New York: Penguin, 2006.

Zukav, Gary. *The Seat of the Soul*. New York: Simon & Schuster, 1989.

Zukav, Gary. *Soul Stories*. New York: Simon & Schuster, 2000.

Bibliography

'Abdu'l-Bahá. *'Abdu'l-Bahá in London*. London: Bahá'í Publishing Trust, 1982.

Abdu'l-Bahá. *The Divine Art of Living: Selections from the Writings of Bahá'u'lláh, the Báb, and 'Abdu'l-Bahá*. Edited by Mabel Hyde Paine. Revised ed. Wilmette, IL: Bahá'í Publishing Trust, 2006.

Abdu'l-Bahá. *Foundations of World Unity*. Wilmette, IL: Bahá'í Publishing Trust, 1945.

'Abdu'l-Bahá. *Paris Talks: Addresses Given by 'Abdu'l-Bahá in Paris in 1911*. London: Bahá'í Publishing Trust, 1995.

'Abdu'l-Bahá. *Promulgation of Universal Peace: Talks Delivered by 'Abdu'l-Bahá during His Visit to the United States and Canada in 1912*. Compiled by Howard MacNutt. 2nd ed. Wilmette, IL: Bahá'í Publishing Trust, 1982.

'Abdu'l-Bahá. *The Secret of Divine Civilization*. Translated by Marzieh Gail. Wilmette, IL: Bahá'í Publishing Trust, 1957.

'Abdu'l-Bahá. *Selections from the Writings of 'Abdu'l-Bahá*. Compiled by the Research Department of the Universal House of Justice. Translated by a committee at the Bahá'í World Center and Marzieh Gail. Haifa: Bahá'í World Center, 1978.

'Abdu'l-Bahá. *Some Answered Questions*. Compiled and translated by Laura Clifford Barney. Revised ed. Wilmette, IL: Bahá'í Publishing Trust, 2014.

'Abdu'l-Bahá. *Star of the West, Vol. 1: 1910–1911.* http://starofthewest.info.

'Abdu'l-Bahá. *Star of the West, Vol. 8: 1915–1917.* http://starofthewest.info.

'Abdu'l-Bahá. *Star of the West, Vol. 9: 1918–1919.* http://starofthewest.info.

'Abdu'l-Bahá. *Star of the West, Vol. 13: 1922–1923.* http://starofthewest.info.

'Abdu'l-Bahá. *Star of the West, Vol. 17: 1926–1927.* http://starofthewest.info.

'Abdu'l-Bahá. *Tablets of 'Abdu'l-Bahá Abbás.* Chicago: Bahá'í Publishing Committee, 1909.

'Abdu'l-Bahá. *A Traveller's Narrative.* Translated by Edward G. Browne. Cambridge: University Press, 1891.

'Abdu'l-Bahá. *Will and Testament of 'Abdu'l-Bahá.* Read January 3, 1922. https://www.bahai.org/library/authoritative-texts/abdul-baha/will-testament-abdul-baha/will-testament-abdul-baha.pdf?feab4b36.

Afrúkhtih, Yúnis Khán. *Khátirát-i-Nuh-Sálih* [Memoirs of Nine Years]. Translated by Riaz Masrour. Oxford: George Ronald, 1952.

"Anne Morrow Lindbergh: 'It Is Terribly Amusing How Many…'" AZQuotes.com. Accessed July 14, 2020. https://www.azquotes.com/quote/583300.

"Arlene Francis: 'Trouble Is a Sieve Through Which…'" AZQuotes.com. Accessed July 14, 2020. https://www.azquotes.com/quote/542258.

The Báb. *Selections from the Writings of the Báb.* Compiled by the Research Department of the Universal House of Justice. Translated by Habib Taherzadeh. Haifa: Bahá'í World Centre, 1976.

Bahá'í Prayers: A Selection of Prayers Revealed by Bahá'u'lláh, the Báb, and 'Abdu'l-Bahá. 2018 ed. Wilmette, IL: Bahá'í Publishing Trust.

The Bahá'í World, Vol. 2 (1926–1928). New York: Bahá'í Publishing Committee, 1928.

The Bahá'í World, Vol. 5 (1932–1934). New York: Bahá'í Publishing Committee, 1936.

The Bahá'í World, Vol. 12 (1950–1954). Wilmette, IL: Bahá'í Publishing Trust, 1956.

Bahá'í World Faith: Selected Writings of Bahá'u'lláh and 'Abdu'l-Bahá. Wilmette, IL: Bahá'í Publishing Trust, 1976.

Bahá'u'lláh. *Gleanings from the Writings of Bahá'u'lláh*. Translated by Shoghi Effendi. Wilmette, IL: Bahá'í Publishing Trust, 1988.

Bahá'u'lláh. *The Hidden Words*. Translated by Shoghi Effendi. Wilmette, IL: Bahá'í Publishing Trust, 2003.

Bahá'u'lláh. *The Kitáb-i-Aqdas*. Haifa: Universal House of Justice, 1992.

Bahá'u'lláh. *Prayers and Meditations by Bahá'u'lláh*. Translated by Shoghi Effendi. Wilmette, IL: Bahá'í Publishing Trust, 1988.

Bahá'u'lláh. *The Seven Valleys and the Four Valleys*. Translated by Marzieh Gail. Wilmette, IL: Bahá'í Publishing Trust, 1991.

Bahá'u'lláh. *Tablets of Bahá'u'lláh Revealed after the Kitáb-i-Aqdas*. Translated by Habib Taherzadeh. Wilmette, IL: Bahá'í Publishing Trust, 1988.

"Barbara Holland Quotes." AZQuotes.com. Accessed July 14, 2020. https://www.azquotes.com/author/23641-Barbara_Holland.

Breathnach, Sarah B. *Simple Abundance: A Day Book of Comfort and Joy*. New York: Time Warner, 1995.

Campbell, Joseph. *Reflections on the Art of Living: A Joseph Campbell Companion*. Reprint ed. Edited by Diane K. Osbon. New York: Harper Perennial, 1995.

Dusay, Jack. *Egograms: How I See You and You See Me*. New York: Harper and Row, 1977.

English, Fanita. "The Substitution Factor: Rackets and Real Feelings." *Transactional Analysis Journal* 1, no. 4 (1971): 225–30.

Ernst, Franklin. "Okay Corral: The Grid for Get-on-With." *Transactional Analysis Journal* 1, no. 4 (1971): 33–42.

Fassler, Joe. "The Stubborn Gladness of Elizabeth Gilbert's Favorite Poet." *The Atlantic*, November 6, 2013. https://www.theatlantic.com/entertainment/archive/2013/11/the-stubborn-gladness-of-elizabeth-gilberts-favorite-poet/281158/.

Furútan, 'Alí-Akbar, comp. and ed. *Stories of Bahá'u'lláh*. Translated by Katayoon and Robert Crerar. Oxford: George Ronald, 1986.

Garcia, Felipe. "Responsivity." *Transactional Analysis Journal* 21, no. 4 (1991): 212–17.

Gilbert, Elizabeth. "Choosing Curiosity over Fear." *On Being with Krista Tippett* (podcast), July 7, 2016. https://onbeing.org/programs/elizabeth-gilbert-choosing-curiosity-over-fear-may2018/.

"George Eliot > Quotes / Quotable Quotes." Goodreads.com. Accessed July 14, 2020. https://www.goodreads.com/quotes/619-it-is-never-too-late-to-be-what-you-might.

Grundy, Julia M. *Ten Days in the Light of 'Akká*. Wilmette, IL: Bahá'í Publishing Trust, 2000.

Honnold, Annamarie, ed. *Vignettes from the Life of 'Abdu'l-Bahá*. Revised ed. Wilmette, IL: Bahá'í Publishing Trust, 1979.

Hatcher, John S. *Understanding Death: The Most Important Event of Your Life*. Wilmette, IL: Bahá'í Publishing, 2009.

Hornby, Helen, comp. *Lights of Guidance: A Bahá'í Reference File*. New Delhi: Bahá'í Publishing Trust, 1988.

Ives, Howard Colby. *Portals to Freedom*. Oxford: George Ronald, 1983.

James, Muriel, and Dorothy Jongeward. *Born to Win: Transactional Analysis with Gestalt Experiments*. Reading, MA: Addison-Wesley, 1996.

Julian of Norwich. *Revelations of Divine Love*. Translated by Elizabeth Spearing. London: Penguin Classics, 1998.

Loving v. Virginia. Oyez. Accessed August 19, 2020. https://www.oyez.org/cases/1966/395.

Rabbání, Rúhíyyih (Mary Maxwell Rabbání). *The Priceless Pearl*. London: Bahá'í Publishing Trust, 1969.

"Rainer Marie Rilke > Quotes > Quotable Quote." Goodreads.com. Accessed July 14, 2020. https://www.goodreads.com/quotes/111325-there-is-only-one-journey-going-inside-yourself.

Redman, Earl. *'Abdu'l-Bahá in Their Midst*. Oxford: George Ronald, 2011.

Rilke, Ranier Maria. *Letters to a Young Poet*. Translated by M. D. Herter Norton. Revised ed. New York: W. W. Norton, 1993.

Rumi, Jalaluddin. "The Guest House." In *The Illustrated Rumi*, trans. Coleman Barks, illus. Michael Green. Broadway Books: New York, 1997.

Scudder, Horace E., ed. *The Complete Poetic and Dramatic Works of Robert Browning*. Cambridge ed. New York: Houghton, Mifflin & Co., 1895.

Shoghi Effendi. *Advent of Divine Justice*. Wilmette, IL: Bahá'í Publishing Trust, 1990.

Shoghi Effendi. *Directives from the Guardian*. Wilmette, IL: Bahá'í Publishing Trust, 1973.

Shoghi Effendi. *God Passes By*. Wilmette, IL: Bahá'í Publishing Trust, 1985.

Shoghi Effendi. "Living the Life." In *Compilation of Compilations, Vol 2*. Compiled by Research Department of the Universal House of Justice, 1–28. Mona Vale: Bahá'í Publications Australia, 1991. http://bahai-library.com/compilation_compilations_2.

Shoghi Effendi. *Unfolding Destiny*. London: Bahá'í Publishing Trust United Kingdom, 1981.

Snyder, Kim A., dir. *I Remember Me*. New York, NY: Zeitgeist Films, 2001.

Spitz, Rene A. "Hospitalism: An Inquiry into the Genesis of Psychiatric Conditions in Early Childhood." *The Psychoanalytic Study of the Child* 1, no. 1 (1945): 53–74.

Steiner, Claude. "The Stroke Economy." *Transactional Analysis Journal* 1, no. 3 (1971): 9–15.

Stewart, Ian, and Vann Joines. *TA Today: A New Introduction to Transactional Analysis*. Nottingham: Lifespace Publishing, 1987.

Taherzadeh, Adib. *The Covenant of Bahá'u'lláh*. Oxford: George Ronald, 1992.

Universal House of Justice, comp. *The Compilation of Compilations: 1963–1990*. 2 vols. Victoria: Bahá'í Publications Australia, 1991.

Universal House of Justice. *Wellspring of Guidance: Messages 1963–1968*. Wilmette, IL: Bahá'í Publishing Trust, 1970.

Willcox, Gloria. *Feelings: Converting Negatives to Positives*. Kearney, NE: Morris Publishing, 2001.

Willcox, Gloria. "The Feeling Wheel: A Tool for Expanding Awareness of Emotions and Increasing Spontaneity and Intimacy." *Transactional Analysis Journal* 12, no. 4 (1982): 274–76.

Williamson, Marianne. *A Return to Love: Reflections on the Principles of a Course in Miracles*. New York: Harper Collins, 1992.

Zinker, Joseph. *In Search of Good Form: Gestalt Therapy with Couples and Families*. Cleveland: Gestalt Institute Publications, 1994.

About the Author

Farzaneh (Fafar) Guillebeaux (M.A., M.S.) is a semi-retired psychotherapist with a specialty in Marriage and Family Therapy. She has conducted national and international training since 1988 in the areas of overcoming racism and sexism, the empowerment of women, inter-racial/intercultural marriage, communication skills, and conflict resolution. She has also presented at the Parliament of World Religions and at the first Sino-American Conference on Women's Issues in Beijing, China. Born in Iran, Fafar—a fifth generation Bahá'í—has lived in the United States for more than 50 years. This book is a result of her deep compassion and commitment to the ideas of spiritual transformation, birthed from her lifetime of personal and professional experience and guided by the principles of the Bahá'í Faith.

www.ingramcontent.com/pod-product-compliance
Lightning Source LLC
Chambersburg PA
CBHW070639050426
42451CB00008B/225